D0065090

*f*P

ALSO BY PETER SIMS

True North:
Discover Your Authentic Leadership

Little Bets

HOW BREAKTHROUGH IDEAS EMERGE
FROM SMALL DISCOVERIES

Peter Sims

FREE PRESS
New York   London   Toronto   Sydney   New Delhi

Free Press
A Division of Simon & Schuster, Inc.
1230 Avenue of the Americas
New York, NY 10020

First Free Press hardcover edition April 2011.

FREE PRESS and colophon are trademarks of Simon & Schuster, Inc.

For information about special discounts for bulk purchases,
please contact Simon & Schuster Special Sales at 1-866-506-1949
or business@simonandschuster.com.

The Simon & Schuster Speakers Bureau can bring authors to your live event.
For more information or to book an event, contact the Simon & Schuster Speakers
Bureau at 1-866-248-3049 or visit our website at www.simonspeakers.com.

DESIGNED BY ERICH HOBBING

Manufactured in the United States of America

9   10   8

Library of Congress Cataloging-in-Publication Data

Sims, Peter.
Little bets : how breakthrough ideas emerge
from small discoveries / by Peter Sims.
    p.   cm.
Includes bibliographical references and index.
1. Success in business.   2. Creative ability.   I. Title.
HF5386.S546 2011
658.4'09—dc22   2010046641

ISBN 978-1-4391-7042-7
ISBN 978-1-4391-7044-1 (ebook)

For my parents—
it all began with a little bet.

Contents

Little Bets

Introduction

Chris Rock has become one of the most popular comedians in the world and, while there is no doubt he has great talent, his brilliance also comes from his approach to developing his ideas. The routines he rolls out on his global tours are the output of what he has learned from thousands of *little bets*, nearly all of which fail.

When beginning to work on a new show, Rock picks venues where he can experiment with new material in very rough fashion. In gearing up for his latest global tour, he made between forty and fifty appearances at a small comedy club, called Stress Factory, in New Brunswick, New Jersey, not far from where he lives. In front of audiences of, say, fifty people, he will show up unannounced, carrying a yellow legal note pad with ideas scribbled on it. "It's like boxing training camp," Rock told the *Orange County Register.*

When people in the audience spot him, they start whispering to one another. As the waitstaff and other comedians find places to stand at the sides or back, the room quickly fills with anticipation. He won't launch into the familiar performance mode his fans describe as "the full preacher effect," when he uses animated body language, pitchy and sassy vocal intonations, and erupting facial expressions. Instead, he will talk with the audience in an informal, conversational style with his notepad on a stool beside him. He watches the audience intently, noticing heads nodding, shifting body language, or attentive pauses, all clues as to where good ideas might reside.

In sets that run around forty-five minutes, most of the jokes fall flat. His early performances can be painful to watch. Jokes will ramble, he'll lose his train of thought and need to refer to his notes, and some audience members sit with their arms folded, noticeably unimpressed. The audience will laugh about his flops—laughing at him, not with him. Often Rock will pause and say, "This needs to be fleshed out more if it's gonna make it," before scribbling some notes. He may think he has come up with the best joke ever, but if it keeps missing with audiences, that becomes his reality. Other times, a joke he thought would be a dud will bring the house down. According to fellow comedian Matt Ruby, "There are five to ten lines during the night that are just ridiculously good. Like lightning bolts. My sense is that he starts with these bolts and then writes around them."

For a full routine, Rock tries hundreds (if not thousands) of preliminary ideas, out of which only a handful will make the final cut. A successful joke often has six or seven parts. With that level of complexity, it's understandable that even a comedian as successful as Chris Rock wouldn't be able to know which joke elements and which combinations will work. This is true for every stand-up comedian, including the top performers we tend to perceive as creative geniuses, like Rock or Jerry Seinfeld. It's also true for comedy writers. The writers for the humor publication the *Onion*, known for its hilarious headlines, propose roughly six hundred possibilities for eighteen headlines each week, a 3 percent success rate. "You can sit down and spend hours crafting some joke that you think is perfect, but a lot of the time, that's just a waste of time," Ruby explains. This may seem like an obvious problem, but it's a mistake that rookie comedians make all the time.

By the time Rock reaches a big show—say an HBO special or an appearance on David Letterman—his jokes, opening, transitions, and closing have all been tested and retested rigorously. Developing an hour-long act takes even top comedians from six months to a year. If comedians are serious about success, they get on stage every night they can, especially when developing new material. They typically do so at least five nights per week, sometimes up to seven, and sweat over every element and word. And the cycle repeats, day in, day out.

Most people are surprised that someone who has reached Chris Rock's level of success still puts himself out there in this way, willing to fail night after night, but Rock deeply understands that ingenious ideas almost never spring into people's minds fully formed; they emerge through a rigorous experimental discovery process. As Matt Ruby says of Rock's performances, "I'm not sure there's any better comedy class than watching someone that good work on material at that stage. More than anything, you see how much hard work it is. He's grinding out this material."

The seed of this book was planted while I was attending Stanford Business School. One of the most common things I would hear people say was that they would do something new—take an unconventional career path or start a company—but that they needed a great idea first. I had worked before then as a venture capital investor, and in that work, I had learned that *most successful entrepreneurs don't begin with brilliant ideas—they discover them.*

Ironically, this would include the biggest business idea to come out of Stanford in decades. Google founders Larry Page and Sergey Brin didn't set out to create one of the fastest-growing startup companies in history; they didn't even start out seeking to revolutionize the way we search for information on the web. Their first goal, as collaborators on the Stanford Digital Library Project, was to solve a much smaller problem: how to prioritize library searches online.

In working through possibilities for doing so, their clever innovation was to realize that the best way to prioritize the results was to measure how many other citations referred to a source. In the academic world, work is often judged by the number of other papers or books that cite it. So, if you wanted to search for books about Joan of Arc, the Joan of Arc book that was cited the most by other Joan of Arc sources would appear first. This insight was the core of their now famous PageRank algorithm.

Yet, even after they realized how powerful their search algorithm was and formulated their much more ambitious goal to "organize all the world's information," they still had not identified the company's breakthrough revenue engine. Until 2002, most web advertising sales, including Google's, came from banner ads that would appear at the top of search result pages. Prices were negotiated on a fixed-fee basis such that Google would price ad deals at, for instance, a million dollars and flash the display ad when it deemed appropriate. Borrowing an idea from a company called GoTo.com (renamed Overture), Google then created AdWords, an automated auction-based system that allowed advertisers to display ads next to specific search terms, such as "hockey" or "flowers." This allowed advertisers to target their ads, while the auctions automatically set the exact price that the market would bear across millions of search terms. Within three weeks after Google made this change, the system had produced twice as much revenue as fixed-priced ads produced within that same period, to the great surprise of many, including CEO Eric Schmidt. Once AdWords became the company's flagship product, Google's revenue growth exploded. Page and Brin did not begin with an ingenious idea, but they certainly discovered one.

The pioneering bookseller Amazon also embraces an experimental discovery mentality. Led by founder and CEO Jeff Bezos, Amazon's culture breathes experimentation. Employees there are encouraged to constantly try things and develop new ideas. It's such an important goal of the company to provoke this that whether or not employees are doing so is a part of their performance reviews. Bezos often compares Amazon's strategy of developing ideas in new markets to "planting seeds" or "going down blind alleys." They learn and uncover opportunities as they go. Many efforts turn out to be dead ends, Bezos has said, "But every once in a while, you go down an alley and it opens up into this huge, broad avenue."

Like Chris Rock, Bezos has accepted uncertainty; he knows that he cannot reliably predict which ideas for new markets will work and which won't. He's got to experiment. One such example is a feature the company launched that would compare a customer's entire purchase history with its millions of other customers in order to find the one person with the closest matching history. In one click, Amazon would show you what items that customer purchased. "No one used it," Bezos has said. "Our history is full of things like that, where we came up with an innovation that we thought was really cool, and the customers didn't care."

Other times, they will be pleasantly surprised. When Amazon launched its Associates program, a marketing scheme that allows other websites to earn affiliate fees by sending buyers to Amazon, it quickly exceeded expectations. "Very quickly we doubled down on it as a favored marketing program," Bezos recalled in an interview with *Harvard Business Review*, "and it's continuing to be very successful eleven years later."

Unlike most CEOs, when trying something new, Jeff Bezos and his senior team (known as the S Team) don't try to develop elaborate financial projections or return on investment calculations. "You can't put into a spreadsheet how people are going to behave around a new product," Bezos will say.

This certainly hasn't been easy: Bezos and his team have had to endure significant criticism over the years for failed experiments. As the dot-com era imploded, for example, Amazon experienced a symphony of negativity. In 1999, the company had opened its site to other sellers, such as used booksellers, when it launched Amazon Auctions, competing directly with eBay. But Amazon struggled to integrate Auctions with the core site and it never gained traction with customers. eBay proved too formidable a competitor. Two years later, Amazon had gained only a 2 percent share of the market and management shut down the operation. It was just one of several significant failures. Another was a partnership with Sotheby's. Launched in 1999 and shut down in 2000, it suffered from customer service–related problems from the start. Critics ridiculed the company, calling it "Amazon.bomb" or "Amazon .con." Some Wall Street analysts and investors even called for Bezos to resign.

However, the ultimate outcome has been that Amazon's exploratory mentality has spawned continual breakthroughs, such as Amazon stores, which allows small vendors to sell products on its site, as well as Amazon Web Services (AWS), which includes Elastic Compute Cloud (EC2), permitting third parties to rent storage space on the company's servers. Third-party vendors now account for roughly 30% of Amazon's sales, a key source of the company's impressive growth.

Chris Rock, the Google founders, and Jeff Bezos and his team are examples of people who approach problems in a nonlinear manner using little bets, what University of Chicago economist David Galenson has dubbed "experimental innovators." Galenson has spent years studying groundbreaking creators, delving deeply into their personal histories and work methods, and he has identified two basic types of innovators, which he calls *conceptual* and *experimental*. Conceptual innovators, such as Mozart, tend to pursue bold new ideas and often achieve their greatest breakthroughs early in life. To be sure, there is an important place for such creative geniuses. Yet, as we all know, prodigies are exceptionally rare.

The type of creativity that is more interesting to Galenson, and that is far more common, is experimental innovation. These creators use experimental, iterative, trial-and-error approaches to gradually build up to breakthroughs. Experimental innovators must be persistent and willing to accept failure and setbacks as they work toward their goals.

The great advantage of working in this way is that when trying to do something new or uncertain, we rarely know what we don't know. Most successful creators, from tinkering inventors to songwriters to novelists, understand this. Thomas Edison famously said, "If I find ten thousand ways something won't work, I haven't failed. I am not discouraged, because every wrong attempt discarded is just one more step forward." He learned from more than nine thousand experiments before inventing the light bulb. Get to know the stories of other great inventors and the pattern repeats. Beethoven made music that sounded like everyone else's until he used experiments to gradually differentiate his style from Mozart's established brand of composition. The creative process he adopted, driven by hundreds of little bets, allowed him to explore new styles and forms with audiences. His surviving manuscripts are riddled with pockmarks, corrections, changes, and cross-outs, some so deep that he would even puncture the manuscript paper with his quill. Over time, Beethoven arrived at a highly distinct style, helping to usher in a new period of classical music, the romantic era, distinguished by compositions full of power and intensity.

Experimental innovators like Rock, Brin and Page, Bezos, and Beethoven don't analyze new ideas too much too soon, try to hit narrow targets on unknown horizons, or put their hopes into *one big bet*. Instead of trying to develop elaborate plans to predict the success of their endeavors, they *do things to discover what they should do*. They have all attained extraordinary success by making a series of little bets.

Little Bets is based on the proposition that we can use a lot of little bets and certain creative methods to identify possibilities and build up to great outcomes. At the core of this experimental approach, little bets are concrete actions taken to discover, test, and develop ideas that are achievable and affordable. They begin as creative possibilities that get iterated and refined over time, and they are particularly valuable when trying to navigate amid uncertainty, create something new, or attend to open-ended problems. When we can't know what's going to happen, little bets help us learn about the factors that can't be understood beforehand. The important thing to remember is that while prodigies are exceptionally rare, anyone can use little bets to unlock creative ideas.

Introduction

Because popular perception suggests that only certain people are brilliant creators (so much so that their feats often become mythical), the tremendous value of attaining innovations and creative outcomes through an experimental approach has long been neglected. When someone has the insight to see clearly into the future, as Bill Gates did about the emerging computer industry when he founded Microsoft, pursuing that brilliant vision with unwavering determination can produce remarkable results. However, when uncertainty replaces certainty or when we lack insight, experience, or expertise about problems, experimental innovation is a far better approach.

Bill Gates, for one, doesn't have enough expertise or insight about the problems the Gates Foundation is trying to solve in different parts of the world to know up front where their money will have the greatest impact. He must learn from hundreds of experiments in order to strategize about and prioritize his resources. One of his favorite experiments in philanthropy has been bed nets that prevent malaria. About two million people die from malaria each year, but ten-dollar bed nets that people wear over their bodies as they sleep to prevent being bitten by malaria-carrying mosquitoes have proven to be very effective at preventing the disease.

Most successful entrepreneurs, especially those who start businesses with limited capital, operate in this experimental way when trying new ideas. They think of learning the way most people think of failure. Take Bill Hewlett and David Packard, founders of one of the most innovative companies in modern history. Bill and Dave started Hewlett-Packard without knowing what they would eventually produce; they just knew they wanted to work together and to build a great company.

The entrepreneurial way of operating was the subject of

some fascinating research by Saras Sarasvathy, a professor at the Darden Graduate School of Business at the University of Virginia. She is one of the few researchers to study how entrepreneurs tend to make decisions. One of her studies, titled "What Makes Entrepreneurs Entrepreneurial," started to ripple through Silicon Valley after prominent investor Vinod Khosla, a cofounder of SUN Microsystems, posted a copy of the article on his firm's website along with the note, "First good paper I've seen."

Sarasvathy wanted to understand what decision-making paths expert entrepreneurs take to build a hypothetical business. Her sample included thirty entrepreneurs who had built companies ranging in size from $200 million to $6.5 billion. The founders, who came from a variety of industries, ranging from steel to semiconductors to biotechnology, worked through a seventeen-page problem set during a two-hour period.

Central to Sarasvathy's conclusions is that entrepreneurs and MBA-trained managers (whom she teaches at the Darden School) use two completely different approaches when doing something new. To illustrate this point, she contrasted two ways to cook a meal (both methods require that the chef know how to cook). The first is for a chef to begin with a specific menu, pick out recipes, shop for the ingredients, and then cook the meal in their own, well-equipped kitchen. Each step is known and can be planned sequentially: step A, followed by step B, to accomplish outcome C. Management training emphasizes this procedural planning approach, begin with a predetermined goal and use a given set of means to accomplish that goal in the fastest, cheapest, most efficient way.

Another way to cook a meal, Sarasvathy explained, is for a chef to go into a new kitchen, without having a menu or knowing what ingredients will be there. The chef then has to rummage through cupboards in search of ingredients and piece together a meal, improvising along the way. The result may be great or it may not. The only certainty is that the outcome of the second approach will be less predictable than that of the first approach. But, importantly, entrepreneurs do not try to avoid errors or surprises. They seek to learn from them, just as chefs often arrive at new recipes through improvisation. As Sarasvathy wrote, entrepreneurial plans are "made and unmade and recast through action and interaction with others." Sarasvathy's work highlights that both approaches have their benefits. Both ways of working are valuable, but in different situations: When much is known, procedural planning approaches work perfectly well. When much is unknown, they do not.

For instance, when Howard Schultz launched what would become Starbucks, he modeled the stores after Italian coffee houses, a new concept for the United States. Schultz was definitely onto something, but the baristas wore bow ties (which they found very uncomfortable) while customers complained about the menus being written primarily in Italian as well as the nonstop opera music. What's more, the stores had *no chairs*. The Starbucks experience that emerged from the many refinements and tweaks obviously looks and feels quite different from Schultz's initial concept.

The methods of experimental innovation that I introduce in this book emerged from the study of an unlikely set of sources: from creative artists, to scrappy entrepreneurs, to military strategists, to agile software developers, to the rapidly growing field of design thinking. In researching this book, I wanted to identify the methods that were being used by experimental innovators across a broad array of fields, from stand-up comedy to Pixar's creative processes, to find out how these creative people and organizations meet the challenge of consistently discovering new ideas and bringing them successfully to fruition. For several years, I became immersed in the empirical research on creativity and innovation.

One place my curiosity led me is to Stanford University's Hasso Plattner Institute of Design (known as the d.school). Founded by creativity and innovation masters David Kelley and George Kembel, the d.school is one of the leading institutions in the field, and a hub of creative thinking and doing. Kelley had previously cofounded the renowned consultancy IDEO, the company that developed the first Apple computer mouse. Kembel, who now leads the d.school, became my guide and collaborator, and insights from design thinking permeate this book.

Design thinking provides a set of creative methodologies for solving problems and generating ideas that is based on building up solutions, rather than starting with the answer. The field has been developed and refined over several decades, including at the renowned innovation center Xerox PARC during the 1970s and 80s, then later at such places as IDEO. As enrollment trends at the Stanford d.school show, students are flocking to design thinking to complement their more traditional training. Peter Georgescu, former CEO of ad giant Young & Rubicam, may have said it best: "This is the future."

I also conducted extensive field research at leading companies and with highly creative people, seeking to understand the nuanced inner workings of their work methods and creative processes, as well as the barriers that prevented people and organizations from using them. Through this process, I discovered striking commonalities in the ways these people approached their work. Similar ways of thinking and work methods showed up in the ways that Pixar creates its films, the ways entrepreneurs and savvy CEOs like Jeff Bezos identify and develop new market opportunities, the ways architect Frank Gehry designs new buildings, the ways generals go about counterinsurgency strategy and training, and in the ways stand-up comedians generate new material.

These methods are decidedly *not* ways of just trying a lot of things to see what sticks, like throwing spaghetti against a wall. The most productive creative people and teams are rigorous, highly analytical, strategic, and pragmatic. They do not, though, use a formulaic model that can be followed. The ways of thinking and doing that will be introduced in the rest of the book are not a protocol; they do not add up to a step-by-step process. Rather, they are powerful aides to being productively creative that can free the mind to discover and to develop those discoveries in a wide variety of situations, which each of us can draw upon and adapt to our own situations and challenges.

Fundamental to the little bets approach is that we:

- Experiment: Learn by doing. Fail quickly to learn fast. Develop experiments and prototypes to gather insights, identify problems, and build up to creative ideas, like Beethoven did in order to discover new musical styles and forms.
- Play: A playful, improvisational, and humorous atmosphere quiets our inhibitions when ideas are incubating or newly hatched, and prevents creative ideas from being snuffed out or prematurely judged.

- Immerse: Take time to get out into the world to gather fresh ideas and insights, in order to understand deeper human motivations and desires, and absorb how things work from the ground up.
- Define: Use insights gathered throughout the process to define specific problems and needs before solving them, just as the Google founders did when they realized that their library search algorithm could address a much larger problem.
- Reorient: Be flexible in pursuit of larger goals and aspirations, making good use of small wins to make necessary pivots and chart the course to completion.
- Iterate: Repeat, refine, and test frequently armed with better insights, information, and assumptions as time goes on, as Chris Rock does to perfect his act.

For most of us, adopting this experimental approach requires a significant change in mindset. One reason for this is the way most of us have been taught. Great emphasis gets placed in our education system on teaching facts, such as historical information or scientific tables, then testing us in order to measure how much we've retained about that body of knowledge. Memorization and learning to follow established procedures are the key methods for success. Even when we are taught problem solving, such as solving math problems, the focus is generally either on using established methods or logical inference or deduction, both highly procedural in the way they require us to think. There is much less emphasis on developing our creative thinking abilities, our abilities to let our minds run imaginatively and to discover things on our own. We are given very little opportunity, for example, to perform our own, original experiments, and there is also little or no margin for failure or mistakes. We are graded primarily on getting answers right.

Researchers and commentators have described the problem as an overemphasis on memorization and on left-brain analytical skills. The consequence is, they argue, that our right-brain capacities to create and discover get suffocated. As education and creativity researcher and author Sir Ken Robinson puts it, "We are educating people out of their creativity."

Another major factor is that, for years, organizational management has been developing methods for increasing productivity and minimizing risk and errors that tend to stifle creative experimentation. The predominant approach to management that evolved during the industrial era, known as *scientific management*, broke jobs down into specific, sequential tasks, which could then be allocated appropriate times for completion in order to optimize efficiency. Hierarchical organizations with centralized top-down decision making facilitated this process and became the norm. These methods famously allowed Henry Ford to streamline the automobile production line, first revolutionizing manufacturing and then the service businesses as well. But the emphasis on linear systems, top-down control, relentless efficiency and eradicating failure left little room for creative discovery and trial and error.

We need look no farther than General Motors to understand why the emphasis on sequential processes, regimented systems and detailed planning led to the stifling of innovative capacities, which was largely responsible for bringing GM to the verge of its death. Chet Huber, a retired thirty-seven-year veteran of the company, including as the founding CEO of the GM subsidiary OnStar, looks back on his GM tenure, work, and colleagues with great affection. But he readily acknowledges the company's crippling propensity to overplan. "There were some *complicated* planning diagrams," he shared, his voice peaking with intonations, "There were these *crazy* diagrams where before you even got to the four-phase vehicle development process, there was a preprocess . . . If you put it all together with all the presumed feedback loops, it'd be a hologram that would probably take up a football field." It's not hard to see that with such elaborate, predetermined procedures to follow, employees wouldn't have the opportunity or inspiration to generate new ideas.

Huber is quick to add that GM's emphasis on sequential processes and detailed planning was the outgrowth of a lot of good intention on the part of people who wanted to make GM better. Each piece of a giant GM process diagram represented a place where someone (or some team) added a nugget of wisdom from their experiences. "There would be one more pipe on the drawing because we thought we learned something important out of the last launch cycle or that this was something that got missed, so how do we incorporate it?" Their intention was to prevent mistakes. "It was a very refined, templated process that was meant to refine one hundred years worth of knowledge," Huber recalls. Ironically, in attempting to minimize risk and reduce errors, GM's emphasis on regimented systems stymied innovation. GM was like an aircraft carrier that struggled to maneuver amid increasingly choppy waters.

One key reason for this is that the top-down, procedural planning approach is highly dependent on making predictions about the future based on past experience. GM, for example, emphasized improving on the products and the methods that had worked for it in the past, assuming that demand for its cars and designs would continue.

Throughout the business world, detailed planning became the primary method for trying to predict consumer demand, financial costs, market conditions, and where competition would be coming from. The fact is that much of what we would like to be able to predict is unpredictable. Global market movements, political and cultural complexities, and demographic shifts constantly reshape the ground beneath us. This certainty of uncertainty is becoming ever more evident with the accelerating pace of technological change. The Internet has reduced communications barriers and allows new players from different corners of the world to rapidly emerge and compete globally. Thus, a key flaw with the top-down, central planning approach is how limited it is in allowing us to be limber and able to discover new ways of doing things.

To be sure, experimental innovation should not entirely replace linear thinking in our regular work processes. Engaging in discovery and making little bets is a way to complement more linear, procedural thinking. No one can take their eye off their core business or responsibilities, but anyone can spend a portion of their time and energies using little bets to discover, test, and improve new ideas. In this era of ever-accelerating change, being able to create, navigate amid uncertainty, and adapt using an experimental approach will increasingly be a vital advantage.

The way to begin is with little bets.

CHAPTER 1

Big Bets Versus Little Bets

Perhaps no story I was told while researching this book illustrates the limitations of the conventional, top-down procedural planning approach more vividly than that of Hewlett-Packard. Indeed, the idea to title this book *Little Bets* came from a discussion I had with former HP Executive Vice President Ned Barnholt.

Barnholt is the former CEO of Agilent Technologies, but these days he's one of the more respected executives in Silicon Valley, kind of a senior business statesperson whom people trust. Now in his late sixties, he's a board member at eBay, KLA Tencor, and Adobe. A number of Silicon Valley CEOs consider him a mentor. You wouldn't guess all of this if you met him. Barnholt is a gentle man: genuine, calm, and even tempered. He comes across as grandfatherly.

Before Agilent, the measurement company that was spun off from Hewlett-Packard in 1999, Barnholt worked at Hewlett-Packard for more than thirty years, during which he witnessed and helped build one of the most innovative companies ever. The company had had a remarkable history, averaging 18 percent annual growth from 1939 to 1999 but, by the mid 1990s, the challenges mounted. HP had grown so large, to about $30 billion in sales, that Barnholt and other senior managers felt pinched to reach their double-digit growth goals. The research on innovation identifies this as a common problem for managers as companies grow. Barnholt calls it the *tyranny of large numbers,* explaining that "there's a natural tendency to think in terms of bigger bets as you get to be bigger."

To launch these big new businesses, the company's managers took rigorously logical steps. They worked on numerous initiatives in large, growing markets that were adjacent to or somewhat related to HP's existing business. However, they only looked at opportunities that were *already* billion dollar markets. Barnholt recalls, "Around that time, people said, 'We don't even want to look at opportunities unless it was going to be a billion dollar business.' A billion dollars kind of became a mantra." They then researched and analyzed the markets, segmented them, and developed products. If the idea got far enough, they developed marketing campaigns, sales strategies, and launched them. As Barnholt recalls, "It was very much a deductive, analytical process to identify a grand set of opportunities." Possibilities included areas like flat screen displays, uninterruptable power supplies, or smart utility monitoring of homes. "We had all these ideas. And they were all big," Barnholt recalls, "*but they all failed!*"

Able to grin about it now, Barnholt went on, "The reason they all failed and the reason they were big is that someone was already there." To borrow a phrase from Silicon Valley consultant and author Eric Ries, they "achieved a failure." Their ideas made sense. The technology was great. They executed on their plans well. But they still failed.

HP's assumptions turned out to be wrong because of what Barnholt calls *intangible factors,* the realities beneath the surface: the underlying customer problems, needs, preferences, and supporting market dynamics. They were not discovering new opportunities or developing new products, they were relying on the success of competitors to identify the areas they targeted. They weren't being creative. Barnholt then leaned back in his chair and summed up the experience by saying: "That's how I learned the importance of making a lot of *little bets*."

Ironically, a much more creative discovery and experimental approach to innovation had been central to making Hewlett Packard into a market-leading behemoth. According to HP veterans, including Chuck House, who also coauthored a history of the company called *The HP Phenomenon,* in earlier years, cofounder Bill Hewlett loved to make what he called *small bets* to uncover unpredictable opportunities. That approach helped HP pioneer handheld calculators. In 1972, HP's first calculator, the HP-35, would retail at $400 at a time when the market for scientific calculators did not yet exist. The technology was remarkable and the calculator could fit into your pocket. But the price tag was hefty, especially at a time when the alternative was inexpensive slide rules. People inside HP were torn about what to do. So, they hired SRI International to do some market research. SRI was then considered the premier computing research group. They had done pioneering work for General Electric, RCA, and others. "They knew more about computing than anyone," House recalls, "and they said, 'This thing can't sell.' "

Bill Hewlett wasn't so sure. He had just spent several hours on a plane talking about the HP-35 with the person next to him, who thought it was amazing. Hewlett suggested, "Why don't we build a thousand and see what happens?" It was an affordable bet. Within five months, HP was selling one thousand calculators a day and could barely keep up with the demand.

For many years, when Bill Hewlett and Dave Packard led HP, the company never did traditional market research. Instead, HP got most of its ideas for new products by informally observing or talking with customers to identify problems and needs. HP's first computer, in fact, began as a small bet after customers using HP voltmeters (an instrument for measuring electric circuits) complained about not being able to transcribe the meter's six digital readouts per second. "So, the guys at the [HP] lab said, 'You know, we've heard about these 'computer things.' Suppose they could grab the data?" House recalls. Reflecting on his experiences, Ned Barnholt came to a similar point of view and said, "A lot of our most successful ideas over the years came from the bottom up, by really understanding user needs."

The value of the little bets approach to a company like HP, which must contend with the remarkably fast pace of change in the technology business, may seem obvious. However, consider how the approach is also being used by the U.S. military. Colonel Casey Haskins has got a big job; as head of the Department of Military Instruction at the United States Military Academy at West Point, Haskins has two major responsibilities. First, he oversees the military tactics courses that West Point cadets must take during each of their first three years. The other is West Point's three-month summer training programs for which Haskins and his team construct immersive experiences to prepare cadets for what they'll encounter on the battlefield.

Now in his late forties, Haskins is a West Point graduate and a career Army veteran. With a short tuft of graying hair combed to the left side of his otherwise short-cropped head, he combines significant intellectual breadth with a wry sense of humor that is oddly reminiscent of Jack Nicholson's. He effortlessly pirouettes in conversation from insights about biology to stories about Napoleon to buying a used car to neuroscience. Here's how Haskins described the transformation going on inside the army in order to adapt to demands for more limber, creative operating methods.

During the Cold War, the Soviet Army was extremely formidable, yet also fairly predictable. Soviet officers were educated at traditional military academies and prided themselves on having extremely efficient military operations. "The Soviet doctrine was very clear," Haskins says. "Wherever they find a weakness, they're going to flood in." He compares what a ground war with the Soviet Army would have been like to being in a batting cage. "If the hitter swings and misses, the next pitch comes twice as fast from the pitching machine," he says with a chuckle. "And, if you miss another one, it starts throwing *straight at you!*"

During the Cold War, the Soviets had an absolutely potent and efficient ground force. The Soviet Army possessed tens of thousands of tanks, artillery pieces, and rockets. "So," Haskins relates, "the [U.S.] Army needed to get really, really, really good at fighting those." Any ground war between the U.S. and Soviet armies—what would have been World War III—would have likely been short and catastrophic. "That war was going to be: all the chips on the table. Two weeks. Winner takes all. The whole world is at stake." The army prepared its soldiers accordingly.

One of the main ways the army did this was to require soldiers to essentially memorize checklists. In army terms, these are called "doctrinally approved solutions." Military doctrine enables the army to manage its operations across a large organization. Because fighting the Soviet Army allowed for such a small margin of error, approved solutions detailed how to solve anticipated battlefield problems with precision and efficiency.

For example, since a ground war against the Soviet Army would most likely have been fought in Central Europe, particularly Germany, approved solutions covered things like knowing exactly how much weight each bridge in Germany would support or when and how to tap into a network of underground fuel pipes. Soldiers also learned how to put obstacles in front of Soviet tanks or to jam their radio signals. And so on. All of these tactics were designed to disrupt the Soviet Army just long enough for the U.S. Army to make its own offensive moves. Army personnel, such as cadets at West Point, then repeatedly practiced these approved solutions.

Given the Soviet Army's predictable strategy and tactics during the Cold War, one could make a pretty good case for this strategy and approach. Time would be of the essence and, therefore, there was extremely little room for error. Centralized, top-down decision making and tight controls, driven by doctrine approved solutions, established efficiencies and predictable execution. The Soviet Army would annihilate the U.S. Army on the battlefield if the U.S. Army wasn't almost perfectly in sync. "We were very efficient and mechanized and everyone knew just enough about what they had to know and then they got really in depth at their core competency," Haskins says. "Henry Ford could have designed this system. There would be a few people making decisions and the rest of the people executing them as best as they could."

The army ran into the serious limitations of this approach during the Vietnam War. One of the men in charge of U.S. strategy in the war for many years was Robert McNamara, secretary of defense under Presidents Kennedy and Johnson. McNamara was known for his enormous intellect, renowned for achievements at Ford Motors (where he was once president) and in government. Many considered him the best management mind of his era.

During World War II, McNamara had gained acclaim for developing statistical models to optimize the destruction from bombing operations over Japan. The challenge of Vietnam, however, proved to be different in ways that exposed the limits of McNamara's approach. McNamara assumed that increased bombing in Vietnam would reduce the Viet Cong resistance with some degree of proportionality, but it did not. There wasn't a linear cause and effect relationship. The Viet Cong kept shifting its positions and strategies (including using extensive tunnels), but mostly proved far more resilient than McNamara and the other U.S. planners expected.

McNamara had fallen prey to what I'll call the "illusion of rationality." We are all vulnerable to this illusion. It happens when ideas or assumptions seem logical in a plan, spreadsheet model, PowerPoint, or memo, yet they haven't been validated on the ground or in the real world. The Vietnam War would, of course, ultimately defy McNamara's predictions. He achieved a failure that haunted him for years until, at age eighty-three, he contritely acknowledged, in the 2004 documentary *The Fog of War*, that "War is so complex it's beyond the ability of the human mind to comprehend all the variables."

The wars in Iraq and Afghanistan have again highlighted this challenge. Adaptive guerilla warfare has replaced conventional warfare as the predominant mode of fighting for which the U.S. military must prepare. Unlike the Soviet officers, Middle Eastern insurgent groups, such as al-Qaeda and the Taliban, don't learn tactics at traditional military academies, nor are they centrally coordinated. Amid constantly evolving warfare, it's impossible for soldiers to abide by approved solutions. As Haskins sums up the army's urgent challenge, "Not only can we not teach doctrinally approved solutions any more [which take roughly two years to be approved], the truth is, we don't even know all the problems!"

During the Cold War era, the army focused so much on training highly specific, repeatable tasks and eliminating potential errors, that when it faced the new style of insurgent warfare in the Middle East, many soldiers were utterly unprepared. Systems and approved solutions had become too much of a substitute for moment-to-moment, creative problem-solving. To effectively confront the insurgent enemies of today and the future, soldiers must be able to identify and solve unfamiliar problems, rapidly adapting to the circumstances unfolding on the ground. They work from the ground up and must learn from the environment—the people and the situation in each village and town—then craft new tactics that will address the problems they discover. They must be willing and able to adapt those tactics and keep developing new ones as they go.

So, for example, when soldiers arrive in a new city, they must first learn about the nature of the insurgent enemies by meeting with local tribal elders. Soldiers will actually live inside the city and immerse themselves in the civilian population in order to understand the local power structure and identify the government officials and people from the population at large who will be reliable advisors and informants. They will then experiment with ways to gain more knowledge and control over the situation, such as how the insurgents in that particular area will fight, how strong their will is, what weapons they have, and what tactics they will use. Instead of fighting *with* information, the army must fight to *get* information.

One such experiment used during the Iraq war was to build a nine-foot dirt berm around the city of Tal Afar that was controlled by al-Qaeda insurgents. The army then used three checkpoints to monitor and control the flow of goods and people (namely insurgents) into and out of the city. In addition to gradually isolating the insurgents from their external support, the checkpoints provided surprisingly valuable intelligence and allowed the army's plans to evolve. The army learned, for instance, that insurgents expected a forceful attack on the al-Qaeda-controlled part of town and had planted improvised explosive devices (IEDs) accordingly. So, the army switched its strategy from a full-fledged assault on insurgent positions and, instead, took control of the city block by block.

The counterinsurgency approach is one of discovery and experimentation, a creative approach to warfare. Preconceived templates or plans are obsolete. The cornerstone of counterinsurgency operations is what Army strategists call *developing the situation through action*. Central to the process is acknowledging that mistakes will be made, like violating cultural norms or initially picking the wrong partners, because soldiers are operating in an arena of uncertainty. They must be willing to seize (and retain) the initiative by taking action in order to discover what to do, such as by launching frequent reconnaissance probes. In order to help soldiers become comfortable with this approach, Haskins says, "You have to catch people making mistakes and make it so that it's cool. You have to make it undesirable to play it safe."

To help facilitate this change in thinking, as improbable as it may sound, the army has turned to design thinking. The army's prestigious School for Advanced Military Studies (SAMS), where it trains its best and brightest, even offers courses on what it calls the *art of design*. Design is, in fact, in the middle of the revised U.S. Army's field manual *FM 5-0: The Operations Process*, chapter 3. It reads: "Design is a methodology for applying critical and creative thinking to understand, visualize, and describe complex, ill-structured problems and develop approaches to solve them." As far away from military matters as design may seem to be, with design thinking defined as such, its applicability to the challenges of navigating a mission within an uncertain Middle Eastern city is immediately clear.

Two fundamental advantages of the little bets approach are highlighted in the research of Professor Saras Sarasvathy: that it enables us to focus on what we can afford to lose rather than make assumptions about how much we can expect to gain, and that it facilitates the development of means as we progress with an idea.

Sarasvathy points to the value of what she calls the *affordable loss principle*. Seasoned entrepreneurs, she emphasizes, will tend to determine in advance what they are willing to lose, rather than calculating expected gains. Using a little bets approach facilitates operating according to the affordable loss principle. Bill Hewlett's small bet on manufacturing one thousand calculators is a great case in point of this kind of thinking, especially when contrasted with HP's later quest to go after billion dollar markets.

Her work also shows that entrepreneurs tend to be highly aware of the importance of their means, which she defines as: *Who they are*: their values and tastes; *What they know*: their expertise, knowledge, experiences, and skills; and *Who they know*: their networks, friends, and allies. Of course, we should also add their monetary resources. She highlights that successful entrepreneurs are comfortable being adaptable in pursuit of their larger goals in large part because they are progressively building their means, such as by recruiting people or partners with complementary skills and experiences.

The surprising story of Pixar's development from a struggling startup without a viable business plan into one of the most successful movie makers ever beautifully illustrates both the value of building means as well as an affordable losses mentality.

Pixar was a computer hardware company when Steve Jobs bought it in 1986. Before purchasing Pixar, Jobs had been forced out of Apple in 1985 by his hand-picked CEO successor, John Sculley, following frequent clashes. Sculley wanted Jobs to focus exclusively on products, while Jobs wanted to take Apple back over from Sculley. After Sculley caught wind of an attempted coup by Jobs when Sculley was on a trip to Asia, he stripped Jobs of his responsibilities. Jobs then left Apple, bought Pixar, and started another computer company, called Next Computer. Both Pixar and Next struggled, and the open question was whether Steve Jobs was just another one-hit wonder. Jobs had had a clear initial vision for Next: to provide computer workstations to the education market. That vision would morph over time, as the company tried to penetrate other markets, such as banking, but the company's growth never took off. Ironically, while Next would bomb, Pixar would become a sensational success, but not at all according to an ordained plan. Pixar was a hardware business, a software business, and a digitally animated TV advertising company before it became a full-length feature film company. Ultimately, it was the audacious vision of one of the key members of the Pixar team that ultimately prevailed.

By the mid-1980s, Pixar's lead technologist and president,

Ed Catmull, had long been determined to make a feature-length, computer-animated film. This was not lost on anyone who knew him. Catmull had developed the passion during the mid-1970s when he was a graduate student at the University of Utah. It would be nearly twenty years before Pixar's first animated film, *Toy Story*, was released in 1994.

Catmull's bold vision helped him recruit an ever-growing cast of collaborators with complementary means, including graphics technology specialist Alvy Ray Smith, and John Lasseter, a traditional animator from Disney who had the creative and artistic abilities that Catmull did not. Lasseter brought his expertise about filmmaking processes, such as how to use storyboards to develop a script, or conduct animation reviews that would ultimately shape Pixar's creative processes. As Sarasvathy's work demonstrates, building up means is not only a source of support for ideas, but also a way of guiding adaptations.

Back in the mid-1980s, though, virtually no one took Catmull & co.'s desire to make a feature film seriously. After all, computer-generated graphics were extremely costly and Catmull, Smith, and Lasseter were unproven. At the time, Pixar was a startup within George Lucas' Lucasfilm, and had developed the Pixar Image Computer, which allowed people to visualize complex images clearly, such as CAT scans and MRIs, but they hadn't sold any machines yet. Needing cash while going through a divorce, George Lucas put the division up for sale. Catmull, Lasseter, and about forty-odd employees would go with the division.

Incredibly in retrospect, despite shopping Pixar around to a host of potential investors and acquirers, only one serious buyer remained: Steve Jobs. Jobs, who had recently been ousted from Apple (he would, of course, later return) was looking for something to do. Seeking ideas, Jobs went for a walk with eminent technologist Alan Kay, a classmate of Catmull's from the University of Utah. Kay suggested that Jobs take a serious look at Catmull and his team at Pixar; soon thereafter, Jobs fell in love with the technology. Eventually, George Lucas sold the company to Jobs in 1985 for the rock-bottom price of $5 million (Lucas had originally asked for $30 million).

According to Pixar historian David Price, author of the superb *The Pixar Touch*, although the digital imaging technology captivated Jobs, he did not anticipate that the company would produce revenues from animation when he invested. In fact, the relative importance of animation at Pixar could perhaps be best illustrated by the fact that John Lasseter's desk was situated in a hallway. Catmull had originally justified hiring Lasseter (to George Lucas) so that Pixar could make short animated films to demonstrate the company's imaging hardware.

But Steve Jobs repeatedly decided to allow Catmull to develop his team's ability to make films by green-lighting a series of short films, which we will look at in more detail later, even though Pixar could expect little or no value from them. Thinking in terms of affordable losses, Jobs's decisions made sense. Lasseter's salary was roughly $140,000 per year, and his several assistants likely made a good deal less. Relative to the tens of millions of dollars that Jobs had invested in Pixar by 1988, the animation team was still a minimal cost. Had Jobs instead based his decisions on what he could *expect to gain* from digital animation, he might well have shut the group down early on, especially since no basis for predicting what sort of revenue might ultimately be generated by computer animated films yet existed.

Critically, the short films also allowed Pixar to continue to develop its means, including the company's digital animation expertise, reputation, brand, and ever-improving technology. They also continuously developed the ability to tell a good story. Each short became more emotionally nuanced and graphically realistic as Pixar built increasingly sophisticated software. These progressively developed technology and storytelling means were what convinced Disney to partner with Pixar to make *Toy Story*. It was that partnership that then provided the additional financial, production, and distribution means that Pixar needed to accomplish Catmull's vision. As Price learned, "It was the quality of this body of work, rather than old-boy connections or an isolated break, that had made Pixar the front runner once Disney became interested in the medium [computer animation]." Pixar had finally gained enough storytelling, technology, and animation means, as well as the necessary insight into the problems they wanted to solve.

Determining what he can afford to lose is also what Chris Rock does when going before audiences with rough material. One might think that Rock would worry about letting himself bomb in front of people, lest it damage his reputation. He figures that even if some people do leave his experimental appearances disillusioned, and audience members will fold their arms in disappointment or jeer, it's an affordable loss. Not only will most of the people appreciate the chance to see his creative process in action, he also knows that those "losses" are contributing to the larger payoff of a highly successful show that will be seen by millions.

Of course the subject of affordable losses highlights a key issue with the little bets approach—it inevitably involves failure. In almost any attempt to create, failure, and often a good deal of it, is to be expected. Bill Hewlett's approach to identifying new opportunities using small bets did not come without numerous failures. In 1971, HP featured over 1,600 products in its catalog, none of which averaged sales of more than ten units per day, according to Chuck House. In fact, Hewlett estimated that roughly only six out of every 100 new HP products would become breakout successes.

In investigating what facilitates the successful practice of little bets, a certain way of thinking about failure plays an important role. Successful experimental innovators, as we'll next explore, tend to view failure as both inevitable and instrumental in pursuing their goals. Just think about Chris Rock allowing himself to bomb night after night in order to get those few laughs that show him the way forward. Let's dig a bit deeper to understand how experimental innovators think about failure.

CHAPTER 2

The Growth Mind-set

By advocating the little bets approach, I am in no way arguing against bold ambition. Ambitious (dare I employ the over-
used word audacious) goals are essential. Jeff Bezos, Chris
Rock, and the Google founders would never have done anything great without them. A big vision provides the direction
and inspiration through which to channel aspirations and
ideas. But one of the most important lessons of the study of
experimental innovators is that they are not rigid in pursuit
of that vision, and that they persevere through failures, often
many of them. When they run into problems, they accept that
they must go down some unexpected paths in order to get to
the ultimate goal, or maybe even redefine what that ultimate
goal should be. This requires being willing to walk away from
ideas that seemed great, overcoming significant challenges, as
well as coping with the emotional impact of failure. This is, of
course, much easier said than done.

One of the striking characteristics of those who have
learned to practice experimental innovation is that, like Chris
Rock, they understand (and come to accept) that failure, in
the form of making mistakes or errors, and being imperfect is

essential to their success. It's not that they intentionally try to fail, but rather that they know that they will make important discoveries by being willing to be imperfect, especially at the initial stages of developing their ideas. An essential part of the Silicon Valley ethos is that the culture there embraces a willingness to fail in order to learn what to do, something SUN Microsystems cofounder Vinod Khosla has described well: "I believe in bumbling around long enough to not give up at things. And eventually success comes your way, because you tried to fail in every possible way, the only way that's left is the one successful way, and always, for entrepreneurs, seems to come last. It's so obvious when it comes."

By expecting to get things right at the start, we block ourselves psychologically and choke off a host of opportunities to learn. In placing so much emphasis on minimizing errors or the risk of any kind of failure, we shut off chances to identify the insights that drive creative progress. Becoming more comfortable with failure, and coming to view false starts and mistakes as opportunities opens us up creatively. Some fascinating research illuminates why some people have a more resilient approach to failure than others, as well as how to cultivate a more constructive frame of mind about the inevitable failure that accompanies learning.

Dr. Carol Dweck, a professor of social psychology at Stanford University, is one of the leading experts on why some people are more willing (and able) to learn from setbacks. Based until 2004 at Columbia University, Dweck has studied motivation for several decades. Her research has demonstrated that people tend to lean toward one of two general ways of thinking about learning and failure, though everyone exhibits both to some extent. Those favoring a fixed mind-set believe that abilities and intelligence are set in stone, that we have an innate set of talents, which creates an urgency to repeatedly prove those abilities. They perceive failures or setbacks as threatening their sense of worth or their identity. Every situation, therefore, gets closely evaluated: "Will I succeed or fail? Will I look smart or dumb? Will I be accepted or rejected?" Fixed mind-sets cause people to be overconcerned with seeking validation, such as grades, titles, or social recognition. Conversely, those favoring a growth mind-set believe that intelligence and abilities can be grown through effort, and tend to view failures or setbacks as opportunities for growth. They have a desire to constantly challenge and stretch themselves.

Michael Jordan is one of Dweck's oft-used examples of someone with a growth mind-set. He did not start out as a player who would obviously become one of the greatest ever in his game. Rather, he exerted enormous effort to reach that level, and even after having attained it, he continued to work extremely hard. So, for example, even as one of the top NBA players, Jordan worked to improve his three-point range shooting. After shooting 18 percent or less during his first four seasons, Jordan ended his thirteen-year career at an average of 33 percent. He was fiercely competitive but, win or lose, he was honest with himself and constantly sought to build his capabilities. "If you try to shortcut the game, then the game will shortcut you," Jordan said. "If you put forth the effort, good things will be bestowed upon you."

Meanwhile, Dweck describes John McEnroe as exemplifying someone with a fixed mind-set. If he started losing a tennis match, he would blame everyone in sight for the problem, from line judges to people in the stands. Rather than making adjustments to refocus and improve his game, he became distracted and angry (and notorious for his temper tantrums).

Dweck is quick to note that people with a fixed mind-set

can be quite confident, just as John McEnroe was when he was winning. She says, "You can be very confident in a fixed mind-set, but every time you hit a setback, every time you have to struggle, every time other talented people come around, one has to guard against that threatening information." As such, Dweck says it's difficult to maintain confidence in a fixed mind-set without distorting the world, such as acting defensively or blaming someone or something else for setbacks.

Dweck initially developed the fixed versus growth mind-set distinction by studying how schoolchildren reacted to failure and challenges. To her surprise, she found that some students relished difficulty and challenge. "I love a challenge," a student might say. Or if he got a low grade on an exam he might react, "I need to try harder next time." Alternatively, if a child leans toward a fixed mind-set, a low grade would cause him to question his intelligence or worth. He'd say things like, "I feel like a reject," or, "I'm the most unlucky person on earth."

Dozens of studies later, Dweck's findings suggest that people exhibiting fixed mind-sets tend to gravitate to activities that *confirm* their abilities, whereas those with growth mind-sets tend to seek activities that *expand* their abilities. Dweck explains, "When confronted with a task, people with a fixed mind-set ask, 'Am I going to be good at it immediately?' With a growth mind-set, people ask, 'Well, can I learn to do it?' " Students with fixed mind-sets want to appear capable, even if that means not learning in the process. Because setbacks and criticism threaten their self-image, they give up more easily and exhibit greater risk aversion.

People with a growth orientation, on the other hand, are willing to take more risks since challenging experiences represent chances to grow. They don't believe their performance on every task reflects on their intelligence. Dweck sums up the point this way: "The bottom line is that the fixed mind-set makes it hard to maintain confidence because difficulty, effort, and other people who are perceived to be better all pose threats. But, in a growth mind-set, the same things are opportunities."

One of the most important discoveries in Dweck's research is that a person's mind-set can be strongly influenced by what he is led to think is more important: ability or effort. Her formative work focused on a series of studies with four hundred fifth-grade students. Initially, students were given a set of puzzles, easy enough for anyone to solve. Afterward, they were randomly divided into groups. One group was praised for their abilities by being told, "Wow, you got x number correct. That's a really good score. You must be smart at this." Others were praised for their effort: "You must have worked really hard." During the next round, students were given a choice of different tasks: They could either choose an easier task or a challenging task from which they could learn a lot. It turned out that a majority of those praised for their intelligence chose the easier task while up to 90 percent of the students who were praised for their effort chose the challenging task.

In the next phase, students were given hard problems on which they would not be able to do as well. Afterwards, they were told that they had done a lot worse than on the first puzzle, and then were asked for their reactions. The students who had been praised for their efforts not only did better than those praised for their intelligence, they liked the more difficult task even though their results were worse. They did not think their performance reflected upon their intelligence and wanted to take the problems home with them. In the study summary,

Dweck wrote, "The students praised for effort were able to keep their intellectual self-esteem in the face of setbacks."

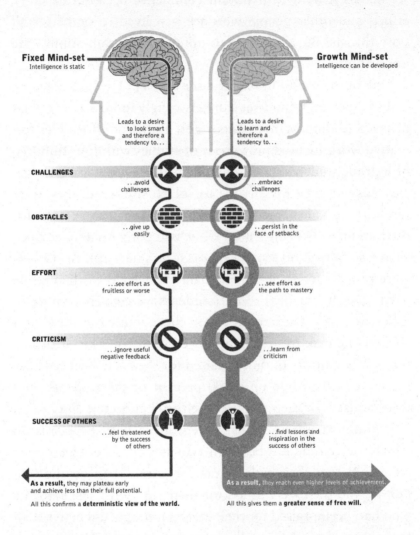

Fixed Mind-set
Intelligence is static

Growth Mind-set
Intelligence can be developed

Leads to a desire to look smart and therefore a tendency to. . .

Leads to a desire to learn and therefore a tendency to. . .

CHALLENGES
. . .avoid challenges
. . .embrace challenges

OBSTACLES
. . .give up easily
. . .persist in the face of setbacks

EFFORT
. . .see effort as fruitless or worse
. . .see effort as the path to mastery

CRITICISM
. . .ignore useful negative feedback
. . .learn from criticism

SUCCESS OF OTHERS
. . .feel threatened by the success of others
. . .find lessons and inspiration in the success of others

As a result, they may plateau early and achieve less than their full potential.

As a result, they reach even higher levels of achievement.

All this confirms a **deterministic view of the world.**

All this gives them a **greater sense of free will.**

On the other hand, the students initially praised for their intelligence performed significantly worse on the harder test and had nearly the opposite reaction to the results. They did not want to take the problems home to practice and the experience caused them to doubt their intelligence. Dweck wrote, "The students who had been praised for their intelligence received an initial boost to their egos, but their view of themselves was quickly shaken when the going got rough." What's more, greater than 40 percent of the group lied about their score to improve it (few students praised for their effort lied). All of this implied that when students were valued for their intelligence, failures would be taken more personally, even as being disgraceful.

Dweck's findings about praise counter broadly held beliefs about developing self-esteem and confidence, but her work has received relatively little criticism. Followup studies, including a meta-analysis of 150 praise studies by scholars at Stanford and Reed College, supported the core findings: Praising ability alone reduces persistence, while praising effort or the processes a person goes through to learn leads to growth mind-set behaviors. Dweck has found this to apply regardless of age.

Once again, Pixar is a great example; the company's management philosophy is thoroughly premised on having a growth mind-set. Pixar's top managers demonstrate a relentless desire to challenge and learn and they ensure that this trickles throughout the rest of the company. "People will frequently disagree with me and frequently I am wrong," says Ed Catmull, who people describe as Pixar's pope or spiritual leader. "If they disagree with me or with John Lasseter or with the directors, the directors don't take that personally." Catmull is even known to ask the company's janitors what they think of Pixar's work and why. There's no penalty for criticizing the work. "And because there's not a penalty, people are more likely to say what they think," he offers.

Perhaps no story I heard about Pixar exemplifies the growth mind-set at the company as clearly as that of the making of *The Incredibles*. When Pixar recruited Brad Bird as a director, Bird was coming off directing a Warner Brothers film called *The Iron Giant* that was a box-office disappointment. Pixar, meanwhile, already had three big hits. Yet Catmull, Steve Jobs, and John Lasseter (Pixar's creative lead) told Bird, "The only thing we're afraid of is complacency—feeling like we have it all figured out. We want you to come shake things up. We will give you a good argument if we think what we're doing doesn't make sense, but if you can convince us, we'll do things in a different way," Bird told Stanford professors Robert Sutton and Hayagreeva Rao. "For a company that has had nothing but success to invite a guy who had just come off a failure and say, 'Go ahead, mess with our heads, shake it up'; when do you run into that?"

Bird would soon test that invitation with his ambitious ideas for *The Incredibles*. His vision for the film had so many characters and sets that members of Pixar's technical team believed it would take ten years and cost $500 million to make. "How are we going to possibly do this?" they asked. A determined Bird implemented a number of changes in Pixar's process in order to do so, from which Pixar learned a great deal. In order to help shake things up, one thing Bird did was to seek out people within Pixar whom he described as *black sheep*, whose unconventional views could help find solutions to the problems. "A lot of them were malcontents because they saw different ways of doing things," Bird said. "We gave black sheep a chance to prove their theories, and we changed the way a number of things are done here."

Among those changes, they altered the approach to storyboards and computer graphics standards. For example, they created what Bird called *superelaborate storyboards* that emulated camera movement to show which parts of the images of scenes needed to be perfect (e.g., have fine-grained detail) and which ones didn't. This allowed the animators to focus their efforts more on the aspects of the movie that required the most attention, such as the action scenes, which were the primary drivers of the film's plot.

They eventually made the film for less money per minute than Pixar's previous movie, *Finding Nemo*, despite significantly more complexity, including three times as many sets. "You want people to be involved and engaged," Bird said. "What they have in common is a restless, probing nature: 'I want to get to the problem. There's something I want to do.' If you had thermal glasses, you could see heat coming off them."

Central to Pixar's success in fostering this growth mind-set through the ranks is the company's attitude about failure. Pixar's managers see a host of failures, false starts, and problems as the modus operandi for developing their films. In fact, when Ed Catmull sums up Pixar's creative process, he describes it as going from *suck to nonsuck*. Pixar film ideas begin on rough storyboards that suck until they work through thousands of problems throughout the process in order to take films from suck to nonsuck.

Of course, just failing is not the key; the key is to be systematically learning from failures. To be closely monitoring what's working and what is going wrong and making good use of that information. Despite an unbroken string of eleven blockbuster films, Catmull regularly says, "Success hides problems." Pixar has a culture where the fear of complacency is a strong motivator, where new problems are identified, discussed, and addressed openly.

The 1980s were difficult for Pixar. Steve Jobs deserves enormous credit for his role in funding and driving the company. Despite Pixar's progress with short films, success was far from guaranteed. During this period, Catmull was puzzled by why so many successful companies ultimately failed. "I'm thinking, 'If we're ever successful, how do I keep from falling into the traps these companies are falling into?' " he recalled.

Catmull watched as companies like Evans & Sutherland, a pioneering computer graphics company, and Silicon Graphics lost their lead. Those companies had access to great talent and problems, yet somehow lost their edge. He studied Toyota the most. Today, Catmull sets the tone for a company culture that is unusually open and honest, resembling Toyota's aspiration of constant improvement. (Amazon's Jeff Bezos is another serious student of Toyota and its processes).

As with Toyota's methods, what interests Catmull the most, and appears to motivate his actions, is to constantly identify and solve new problems. Outsiders like Brad Bird are routinely surprised by Pixar's cultural honesty and willingness to be challenged. When Catmull gives a public speech or lecture, what's most noticeable is that he talks about the problems that Pixar has encountered and the mistakes that he has made. Pixar has, for example, nearly burned out its employees on numerous occasions.

The film that led to the greatest challenge at Pixar was *Toy Story 2*. Less than a year before the film was to be released, John Lasseter and colleagues learned that it would need twelve extra minutes of material. There was also a hard stop on the film's release date, so they had to rewrite large parts of the story in two days. Everyone working on the film at Pixar had to run flat out for months on end, causing a number of staff to develop carpal tunnel syndrome. Deep exhaustion set in. One staff member was so tired, he forgot his infant child in the back seat of his car when he arrived at work one summer morning. Fortunately, he remembered the child before too much time had passed. Miraculously, the film was completed on time to rave reviews, but it was a traumatizing experience. It became a teachable moment for the company: Catmull was determined never to let anything like that happen again. As he puts it, "The measure is how we respond to the crises as they happen. We have to be comfortable being uncomfortable."

Catmull acknowledges through his words and deeds that he doesn't know what he doesn't know. When delivering a lecture at Stanford's Computer Science department, he compared trying to build a successful lasting company to a constant creative process. "There is a lot about this process which I find mystifying still," he said, "There's certain things that I think we've got right and certain things we've got wrong."

Pixar is as close to a constant learning organization as there is, with a proven ability to reinvent and a genuine cultural humility owing to Catmull's prolonged and determined efforts to counter the natural human reactions to success by aspiring to proactively seek out and solve new problems constantly, recognizing that he doesn't have all the answers. This is the growth mind-set in action.

One of those I interviewed who impressed me most in exhibiting a growth mind-set was the architect Frank Gehry. Now in his eighties, Gehry is best known for the Guggenheim Museum in Bilbao, Spain, and Disney Concert Hall in Los Angeles. In 1989, he won the Pritzker Prize, a lifetime achievement award considered the Nobel Prize for architecture. So it was surprising when he said, "I don't feel like I'm at the mountaintop. That's the thing that's really interesting. I don't believe in it. I don't believe I'm there." True to the humility of those words, Gehry is an unassuming man in his personal style. Dressed in a dark blue T-shirt that has a dab of paint on the front, he leaned back in his chair, and continued, "I call it a *healthy insecurity*. I'm still searching for something."

Healthy insecurity is the same phrase Gehry uses to describe how he feels when he begins each new project. "I'm always scared that I'm not going to know what to do," Gehry says. "It's a *terrifying* moment. And then when I start, I'm always amazed: 'Oh, that wasn't so bad.' " Imagine that. After so many successful buildings completed and so many accolades, Gehry still worries, at least at the start of a project, that he'll fail.

One of the most important insights about the growth mind-set and the productive attitude towards failure that it entails is that it is *not* about *not caring* about failure. Not even Frank Gehry can inoculate himself from fears of failure. That is almost surely an integral part of the creative process for everyone to some degree, even those who have achieved the most and the most consistently. The key is that we can teach ourselves to think differently about failures and mistakes, seeing them as opportunities for learning and growth.

Of course, practicing a growth mind-set is much easier for those who start out with that orientation than for those brought up to have a fixed mind-set. The good news is that Carol Dweck's research has shown that not only does everyone actually have a mixture of both fixed and growth mind-sets, but the growth mind-set orientation can be developed. Doing so requires being willing to challenge underlying beliefs about abilities and learning. As someone whose own mind-set was fixed for many years, Dweck recognizes that's a gradual process. "Changing a mind-set is not like surgery," she says. "You can't simply remove the fixed mind-set and replace it with a growth mind-set."

That begins when someone becomes aware of which mind-set they lean toward. Simply knowing more about the growth mind-set allows them to react to situations in new ways. So, if a person tends toward a fixed mind-set, they can catch themselves and reframe situations as opportunities to learn rather than viewing them as a potential for failure.

Next Dweck says that people can think about things in their lives that they thought they wouldn't be good at, but eventually were. "Have I confronted things like this before, that looked hard or daunting, but learned step by step how to do it and master it over time?" she asks. If people don't have growth–mind-set evidence from their own lives, they can often find it in other people close at hand, such as a relative or friend. If need be, one can look to role models who exhibit strong growth mind-sets, such as Michael Jordan or Chris Rock.

Another method that Dweck has shown can facilitate a mind-set shift is to focus people on evidence demonstrating the brain's ability to grow its capacities. In one study, low-income seventh graders were broken into two groups. Through a series of eight workshops, both groups learned study and time management skills. One group was then shown evidence from neuroscience research that the brain is like a muscle and that intelligence can be developed, while the control group did standard work. The experimental group was told:

> Many people think of the brain as a mystery. They don't know much about intelligence and how it works. When they do think about what intelligence is, many people believe that a person is born either smart, average or dumb—and stays that way for life. But new research shows that the brain is like a muscle—it changes and gets stronger when you use it. And

scientists have been able to show just how the brain grows and gets stronger when you learn.

That student group was then provided with further detail about how brain capabilities can be enhanced by creating new neural connections:

When you learn new things, these tiny connections in the brain actually multiply and get stronger. The more that you challenge your mind to learn, the more your brain cells grow. Then, things that you once found very hard or even impossible—like speaking a foreign language or doing algebra—seem to become easy. The result is a stronger, smarter brain.

While both groups had experienced significant declines in their math grades entering seventh grade, the students who received the growth mind-set intervention experimental group showed a significant improvement in their performance. Meanwhile, the control group continued to experience declines. "Students were riveted by this information," Dweck wrote in her summary. "The idea that their intellectual growth was largely in their hands fascinated them." Teachers were unaware which workshop students took, yet follow-up assessments indicated that they singled out three times as many students who took the growth mind-set intervention for showing marked improvements in motivation.

Dweck says that developing a growth mind-set takes time and conscious effort. "It's a process. If it's not habitual, then it's hard work to stay in a growth–mind-set mode." She recommends keeping reminders, such as the growth versus fixed mind-set visual, readily available. "I had a landmark, where one day I heard myself say, 'This is hard. This is fun.' " In terms of how long it takes to develop a growth mind-set, Dweck doesn't offer universal rules. "You can act on it pretty quickly, but well-worn emotional reactions take a lot longer. Even now, I don't love failure," she says.

Of course, no one likes failing. But that's not the point. Our creative capacities won't be liberated unless we let go of the subconscious need to always be perfect or have the immediate answer. None of this is easy, and there will inevitably be setbacks but, as Carol Dweck's research shows, a change of perspective can be developed through experience.

This is another reason why the little bets approach can be so effective: It helps us to cultivate an exploratory, growth mind-set. Practicing little bets frees us from the expectation that we should know everything we need to know before we begin. Redefining problems and failures as opportunities focuses our attention on insights to be gained rather than worrying about false starts or the risks we're taking. By focusing on doing, rather than planning, learning about the risks and pitfalls of ideas rather than trying to predict them with precision up-front, an experimental approach develops growth mind-set muscles.

In the chapters that follow, I will introduce a set of core methods that experimental innovators use to free their minds to generate possibilities, get exposure to a broader range of ideas through active discovery, make fruitful progress when a problem threatens to be too challenging, and facilitate the adaptive development of ideas. As we'll see, discovering and developing new ideas can be daunting, even for the most experienced and successful creators. These methods will provide ways of original thinking and acting that run counter to conventional approaches.

CHAPTER 3

Failing Quickly
to Learn Fast

Being rigorous about spotting flaws and continuing to push toward excellence is essential to creative achievement. After all, Chris Rock, the Pixar filmmakers, Frank Gehry, Steve Jobs, and Colonel Casey Haskins are all perfectionists and yet they accept, even welcome, failure as they develop new ideas and strategies. Rock won't appear on national television without perfecting his act, while Gehry was for years frustrated by the imperfections he noticed while watching performances at Disney Hall (he's past that now). Steve Jobs will famously refuse to release a new Apple product, or product enclosure even, until it's as close to perfect as possible. Yet none of them allow perfectionism to paralyze their creative processes, at least not for long.

Depending on the form it takes, perfectionism is not necessarily a block to creativity. A growing body of research in psychology has revealed that there are two forms of perfectionism: healthy or unhealthy. Characteristics of what psychologists view as healthy perfectionism include striving for excellence and holding others to similar standards, planning ahead, and strong organizational skills. Healthy perfectionism is internally driven in the sense that it's motivated by strong personal values for things like quality and excellence. Conversely, unhealthy perfectionism is externally driven. External concerns show up over perceived parental pressures, needing approval, a tendency to ruminate over past performances, or an intense worry about making mistakes. Healthy perfectionists exhibit a low concern for these outside factors.

Striving for excellence in a healthy perfectionist fashion has many benefits. According to Professor Robert Hill of Appalachian State University, who built upon previous perfectionism research with an experiment with students, "The more an individual was prone to striving for excellence, planning ahead, and being organized, they typically had a high level of psychological well-being, life satisfaction, and positive mood." On the other hand, unhealthy perfectionism, he discovered, leads to negative consequences including depression, anxiety, and eating disorders. Hill found that everyone has some combination of both forms of perfectionism, so escaping from the grip of unhealthy perfectionism, while allowing healthy perfectionist impulses to drive us is a delicate balance.

One of the methods that can be most helpful in achieving this balance, in order to embrace the learning potential of failure, is prototyping. What the creation of low cost, rough prototypes makes possible is failing quickly in order to learn fast. As Pixar director Andrew Stanton, director of *Finding Nemo* and *WALL-E*, describes this way of operating, "My strategy has always been: be wrong as fast as we can. Which basically means, we're gonna screw up, let's just admit that. Let's not be afraid of that. But let's do it as fast as we can so we can get to the answer. You can't get to adulthood before you go through puberty. I won't get it right the first time, but I will get it wrong really soon, really quickly."

Failing quickly to learn fast is also a central operating principle for seasoned entrepreneurs who routinely describe their approach as *failing forward*. That is, entrepreneurs push ideas into the market as quickly as possible in order to learn from mistakes and failures that will point the way forward. This is an extremely well-known Silicon Valley operating principle. Howard Schultz's experience building Starbucks illustrates the point. He and his colleagues had to try hundreds of ideas, on everything from nonstop opera music to baristas wearing bowties, to hundreds of different types of beverages before being able to define the Starbucks experience.

The use of prototypes, often the rougher the better, also greatly facilitates overcoming the blank-page problem. Novelist Anne Lamott believes that every good writer writes what she calls *shitty first drafts*. "The only way I can get anything written at all is to write really, really shitty first drafts," Lamott writes in *Bird by Bird*. Just get it down on paper, she recommends. Write like a child, whatever comes to your mind. "All good writers write them. This is how they end up with good second drafts and terrific third drafts."

Lamott learned this approach when she had to write magazine food reviews. After visiting a restaurant several times, "I'd sit down at my desk with my notes, and try to write a review," she recalls. "Even after I'd been doing this for years, panic would set in. I'd try to write a lead, but instead I'd write a couple of dreadful sentences, XX them out, try again, XX everything out, and then feel despair and worry settle on my chest like an x-ray apron." Despair was the right word. "I'm ruined. I'm through. I'm toast. Maybe, I'd think, I can get my old job back as a clerk typist." She'd look in the mirror, remember to breathe, and then sit back down. "Every time, the answer would come: All I had to do was write a really shitty first draft of, say, the opening paragraph."

> So I'd start writing without reining myself in. It was almost just typing, just making my fingers move. And the writing would be terrible. I'd write a lead paragraph that was a whole page, even though the entire review could only be three pages long . . . the critics would be sitting on my shoulders, commenting like cartoon characters. They'd be pretending to snore, or rolling their eyes at my overwrought descriptions . . .

But it worked. Lamott's drafts would be too long, too boring, and too self-indulgent. They were shitty. But the next day, she'd go through them with a colored pen, find a new lead paragraph and a better ending and rewrite it. "It always turned out fine, sometimes even funny and weird and helpful."

At the beginning of any new idea, the possibilities can seem infinite, and that wide-open landscape of opportunity can become a prison of anxiety and self-doubt. This is a key reason why failing fast with low-risk prototypes the way Chris Rock does is so helpful: If we haven't invested much in developing an idea, emotionally or in terms of time or resources, then we are more likely to be able to focus on what we can learn from that effort than on what we've lost in making it. Prototyping is one of the most effective ways to both jump-start our thinking and to guide, inspire, and discipline an experimental approach.

Frank Gehry, for instance, will begin a new building design by literally cutting up, crumpling, and folding pieces of paper or corrugated cardboard with colleagues. Portrayed in the documentary *Sketches of Frank Gehry*, the paper is sturdy enough to be folded into something that resembles a rectangular structure. Soon a rudimentary building comes into view, perhaps standing several feet tall and wide. "Let's look at it for a while," Gehry says, "and be irritated by it." After examining it closely and thinking about it for a while, he'll say, "Let's cut out a piece here," or, "Let's add a space here."

The initial prototype that emerges over an hour or so barely looks like a building, but it's merely a starting point. They have begun and can work quickly and inexpensively to explore dozens of initial possibilities. Staring at it, Gehry smiles and says, "That is so stupid looking, it's great."

Beyond Gehry's large office window is an extensive workspace where the dozens of work-in-progress models sit atop tables. On a typical project, Gehry Partners will try thousands of ideas that usually culminate in between thirty and fifty major models made from cardboard, plastic, Styrofoam or metal. They build inexpensive prototypes in order to think. One large white model looked like a hall or building, while other smaller structures were made with greenish paper, perhaps to serve as small placeholder buildings. For buildings that are closer to completion, the models look like miniatured versions of an actual building, down to small details like seats placed in the interior. Between the rough starting point and final version, most ideas don't make it. They build off what works and feels best to the people involved and, over time, the models and building forms become increasingly defined.

My greatest education about the power of prototyping came during the spring of 2007, when I was invited to Chicago to witness what ultimately turned out to be history in the making. Just a few stone throws from the Chicago River, on the eleventh floor of 233 North Michigan Avenue, a group of about one hundred people, mostly twenty-somethings, worked away, often late into the night, trying to help elect Barack Obama president. This was May 2007, early days in the campaign, a couple of months after it was launched. As one of the few outsiders granted access, I spent a week there, seeking to understand how the operation was getting pieced together. Perhaps biased by movies about presidential campaigns, I expected to encounter an electric atmosphere. Actually, the office felt much like any other, even a bit lethargic. Despite an open floor plan, people mostly worked quietly in their cubicles while senior advisors had small offices around the exterior. Then again, the first Democratic primary was still more than six months away. The walls were bare except for some maps of Iowa, New Hampshire, Nevada, and South Carolina, the first primary states.

What everyone understood extremely well was that for Obama to win, the campaign would have to cast aside the conventional playbook and create a new one. After all, Hillary Clinton's campaign had virtually every conceivable advantage: worldwide name recognition, the support of the Democratic party establishment, and vast fundraising superiority. Obama was surely a David in the race. The gravity of the challenge was not lost on anyone. Despite their determination, even senior Obama advisors confided that time would quickly tell whether the challenge was insurmountable.

More than any other part of Obama's operation, the new media team (responsible for all things Internet) represented the chance to remake the chessboard. Again, this was nearly seven months before the first primary contest. Set up in a corner facing Lake Michigan, the team of eight people spent most of each day laser-focused on their computers. Each person managed a different part of the operation. One managed online partnerships, such as with Facebook or MySpace. Another person was responsible for the campaign blog, while another focused on driving web traffic to the campaign website. This core group represented the hub for the thousands of people who were joining the Obama campaign online each week. Eight people. And, each of them was in his or her early twenties, except one.

One day, word came that Michelle Obama would come to meet the team that afternoon. Seated around a large conference room table, Mrs. Obama first thanked them for their hard work and offered her support, however she could help. Joe Rospars, the twenty-five-year-old who led the team, then began. He was calm, speaking with certitude, and said that the team had a few guiding principles. Most important, their goal was to create a platform that would provide supporters with the information, community, and tools to mobilize around specific activities, including fundraising, communicating campaign messages, and grassroots political mobilization.

However, neither Rospars nor the rest of team knew what would accomplish those goals. Although Rospars and others had previous campaign experience (from Howard Dean's failed 2000 bid for president), they were already operating in new territory. They didn't yet know what they didn't know.

Their philosophy, Rospars explained, was to test a range of different approaches to figure out which would be the most effective. Going around the table, each person took a minute or two to describe what they were working on. One person discussed how emails with video were increasingly popular. Another said he was prototyping mobile phone ringtones which he then demonstrated using his phone. Instead of ringing, it played a line from a well-known Obama speech: "There is not a liberal America and a conservative America—there is the United States of America."

The room paused for a moment.

"Ringtones?!" Mrs. Obama quizzed, with a hint of disbelief, followed by a smile.

Everyone laughed.

"This one probably won't make it," he admitted, also grinning.

By the end of that session, it became clear that this was an impressive undertaking. Each member of the team had expertise in a different area and was constantly tuning their approach. They had a strong mission, were very open to trying new ideas, listened carefully to incoming feedback to improve their ideas, and learned from countless failures, such as ringtones, in order to learn what to do. Far from naïve idealists, they were extremely pragmatic and strategic. They tracked everything they did with data, and moved on from what didn't ultimately seem useful or valuable, such as ringtones. They weren't wedded to their ideas.

While ringtones were a learning experience, their experiments with text messaging would become hugely influential. "Not only did we not have any list [of cell phone numbers] when we started," Rospars recalls, "we had to figure out along the way, what was text messaging good for?" They ended up sending hundreds of thousands of targeted messages to get supporters to campaign events, register to vote, or communicate other key messages. Similarly, online videos ultimately became a large part of the new media effort. By the end of the campaign, nearly 2,000 YouTube videos were viewed more than 80 million times. As Rospar puts it, "You learn from your mistakes as you go."

The same is true at Pixar, where being able to go from suck to nonsuck when developing a new film is a process of ongoing prototyping, a process that facilitates experimentation by the animators as it allows for a rigorous and continual scrutiny of the work in progress, enabling Pixar to practice healthy perfectionism.

In developing a film the team at Pixar creates thousands of storyboards, a huge number of which include ideas that will not be used for the final product. People at Pixar describe storyboards as the "hand-drawn comic book version" of a movie, a blueprint for the characters and actions. Modeled after Disney's old animation techniques, storyboards are three-by-eight-inch sheets of white paper upon which Pixar's story artists sketch ideas. As Joe Ranft, who was one of Pixar's master storyboard artists, described it, "A story artist gets the plan for a scene whether in script form or loose outline, and starts to draw, exploring possibilities, imagining the scene in pictures, making discoveries, and uncovering unforeseen problems, dramatic or logistical."

Interestingly, with each success they've had, they have challenged themselves even more, and in keeping with that, they have used more storyboards: 27,565 on *A Bug's Life*, 43,536 for *Finding Nemo*, 69,562 for *Ratatouille,* and 98,173 for *WALL-E.* That's a striking expression of healthy perfectionism.

The primary venue for monitoring progress with these story boards are story meetings with the film's director. During the story development phase, the meetings happen daily, attended by the director, members of Pixar's in-house story development team, and storyboard artists. At the story meeting the artists give a basic pitch for their ideas. Pointing at each of the storyboards with a wooden stick, "The artist acts out the boards, telling the story and trying to relate the material in the best way," Ranft said. Afterward, the group provides feedback and brainstorms ways to improve the ideas, storyboard by storyboard. "Choices are made, options are eliminated, and new options are put before the story artist for further exploration," Ranft described it. "In a best-case scenario, a clear direction is given to pursue the scene again. Then it's back to the drawing board for another round." They must persist. The story artists continue to rework the storyboards until the scene works. According to Ranft, "Sometimes the first try works, while other times a dozen or more passes are required."

This process of rigorous critique, and even major change, doesn't end once the initial script has been approved and the first version of the film has been created on what are called *reels*. Reels contain the work-in-progress storyboards, combined with a voice track, that are shown internally before Pixar moves to the expensive digital animation phase. "Every time we show a film for the first time, it sucks," Catmull will say. People then email their comments to the director to explain what they liked, what they didn't, and why, and substantial changes are made.

Pixar's experience with *Finding Nemo* in 2001 was just one example. The film came at a critical time for the company, too, since Disney was considering its option to renew its contract with Pixar. And after six years in the movie business, Pixar hadn't had a bust. Disney's CEO, Michael Eisner, was given a sneak preview of how the movie was unfolding nine months before its release. As David Price recounts in *The Pixar Touch*, Eisner emailed the Disney board: "Yesterday we saw for the second time the new Pixar movie 'Finding Nemo' that comes out next May. This will be a reality check for those guys. It's okay, but nowhere near as good as their previous films. Of course they think it is great." Eisner wanted to wait until the film released (and failed) before conducting further negotiations with Steve Jobs about renewing the Disney/Pixar coproduction deal.

Eisner wasn't wrong, per se, at least about the state of the movie itself. *Finding Nemo* needed dramatic improvement. However, his assessment severely missed Pixar's ability to recognize the issues, iterate, and improve. The team, led by director Andrew Stanton, understood the problems, including the fact that the movie had at least one too many plotlines and endured a frantic nine months to fix them.

Finding Nemo's original script called for a series of flashbacks as the movie progressed. This elaborate back story would gradually reveal reasons why Marlin, a clownfish, was so protective of his son Nemo, since Nemo's mother had been killed in a barracuda attack just before his birth. Stanton initially thought that withholding information from the audience would build anticipation and drama. The first flashback showed Marlin losing his family. The second featured Marlin seeing his wife for the first time. By the third, they were married and moving into their new home inside a sea anemone. The fourth showed Marlin as an expecting father and then, finally near the end of the movie, the fifth flashback showed the barracuda attack. But test audiences, including Eisner, weren't biting. "Ultimately what made it fall apart was there was nothing big to reveal at the end; there was no 'aha' or surprise slant to it," Stanton recalled. "By the time you get to the end, you kind of expected what the tragedy was, it was exactly what you thought it was." The team reworked the story by eliminating the flashbacks and inserting the barracuda attacking Nemo's mother at the film's outset. The remaining problems to be fixed then became much more manageable. *Finding Nemo* would, of course, become another huge Pixar hit, validating Ed Catmull's belief that it's better to fix problems than prevent errors.

The point of describing Pixar's elaborate storyboarding process is not to say that we should all implement just such a process on our own. It is not always possible to have such a large group of critics assemble so many times to offer feedback, for example. But finding ways to fail quickly, to invest less emotion and less time in any particular idea or prototype or piece of work, is a consistent feature of the work methods of successful experimental innovators.

On the flip side of the coin, consider Procter & Gamble, a place where careful planning, risk aversion, and forms of unhealthy perfectionism have long been a way of life. That's understandable. P&G has twenty-three billion-dollar brands, such as Tide, Pampers, and Gillette, where doing something new, even changing the color of the packaging, could risk losing more sales than it would gain or negatively impact the brand equity. Thus, for many years, new product ideas were vetted exhaustively before getting to users. "P&G has certainly had a mind-set of being perfectionists," twenty-one-year P&G veteran Chris Thoen, managing director of Global Open Innovation, puts it. "For a long time, we haven't felt very comfortable doing that [prototyping] because it comes back to perfection: When we interact with consumers, it needs to be totally done."

One of the biggest problems with such unhealthy perfectionism is that so much time can pass before actually *doing* anything. Respected former CEO A. G. Lafley wanted P&G to be able to learn faster and better. So, during his tenure from 2001 to 2009, Lafley instituted a number of changes to create a more innovative culture, including encouraging people there to just try things. He sought out leading design thinkers, including David Kelley, cofounder of IDEO and the Stanford d.school, and Rotman School of Management Dean Roger Martin, to help P&G incorporate methods like prototyping into the company. Lafley was so passionate about prototyping he was known to keep prototypes on his desk.

So, for example, rather than perfect new ideas before showing them to potential users, people have started using low resolution prototypes made from duct tape or cardboard, much like Frank Gehry's. Prototyping allows P&G staff to make things in order to think. "How do you let consumers experience it, even if it falls totally apart within five minutes?" Thoen asks:

> The level of feedback you get is so much more valuable and impactful. . . . The problem with showing something to consumers when it's almost totally done, people don't necessarily want to give negative feedback at that point because it looks like, "This company has spent a lot of money already getting it to this stage and now I'm going to tell them, 'It sucks.' " On the other hand, if something hangs together with tape, and it's clear that it's an early prototype, the mindset of consumers often is, "These people still need some help, so let me tell you what I really think about it."

Thoen beautifully describes the value of prototyping: Potential users of ideas are more comfortable sharing their honest reactions when it's rough, just as people at P&G are less emotionally invested in their ideas. "The barrier of getting feedback from the consumer side is lower," Thoen says, "and the barrier for accepting feedback from the company's point of view is lower as well."

By all accounts, Lafley's efforts had an impact. The results spoke for themselves. After Lafley took over P&G as CEO and chairman, the company's market value increased by more than $100 billion and most all of the company's 5 to 7% annual growth was organic. In order to instill a culture of prototyping, P&G has had to confront those deep cultural inclinations for detailed planning and error minimization. Shaking up the P&G culture has been difficult. Executives there have, among other steps, encouraged employees to talk during management reviews about mistakes they made during planning processes and what they learned, rather than what went right.

In a world that prizes answers and solutions, prototyping can be somewhat counterintuitive, placing the emphasis on doing to be able to think rather than thinking in order to do. Discovery doesn't happen in a vacuum, which is why doing things, however imperfectly at first, opens us up creatively.

CHAPTER 4

The Genius of Play

When Frank Gehry describes his process for designing a new building, he emphasizes how much he values being able to play with his colleagues. "I don't think I would do buildings alone anymore," Gehry says, "I've gotten so used to the team to play with." Gehry's not alone. Creating an atmosphere that allows for playfulness and improvisation is one of the most effective ways to inspire the experimentation that leads to the best ideas and insights. In fact, some compelling research has revealed the neurological basis for how improvisation can unleash creativity.

One of the most-referenced studies was performed by Dr. Charles Limb, a medical doctor and associate professor of head and neck surgery at Johns Hopkins University. He placed musicians in an MRI machine with a small piano keyboard. The subjects were then randomly cued to play either structured music (simple C scales) or to improvise a new melody (using an underlying chord structure) as they listened to a jazz quartet. During the structured simple task, a metronome played 120 beats per second, while musicians repeatedly played a simple C major scale. By contrast, during the improvised task, musicians heard a recorded jazz rhythm and were asked to improvise a melody using only C scale notes. Both times Limb measured their brain activity using functional MRI (fMRI) imaging, focusing on which parts of the brain became more or less active.

As Limb hypothesized, when the performers were playing improvised jazz, activity in the prefrontal cortex, the parts of the brain associated with self-censoring or conscious self-monitoring, were deactivated. As Limb wrote in the study summary, "the lateral prefrontal regions, which were deactivated during improvisation, are thought to provide a cognitive framework within which goal-directed behaviors are consciously monitored, evaluated and corrected." In other words, when the performers switched from structured music to improvised jazz, the part of their brain responsible for evaluating and censoring their behavior effectively switched off. As respected neuroscience expert and author Jonah Lehrer described the study, "It was only by 'deactivating' this brain area—inhibiting their inhibitions, so to speak—that the musicians were able to spontaneously invent new melodies."

Improvising unlocks a far more creative state of mind. Kids don't have the self-censoring capacity of their brain well-developed, which helps explain why they will say outlandish things, and also why kids are often extremely creative. Similarly, when the musicians in Limb's study shifted from C scales to improvisation, their brains stopped consciously monitoring and they created new melodies. Scientists compare the state of mind while improvising to meditation or even to REM sleep cycles, when the mind more readily makes creative associations seemingly because it is less burdened by its evaluative side.

Scientists are still in the early days of understanding the

functions of the brain, as well as their use of fMRI imaging. They do believe, however, that activity in the medial prefrontal cortex, the area of the brain right behind the eyes, is linked with self-expression. That area lit up when Limb's subjects improvised. "Jazz is often described as being an extremely individualistic art form," Limb said. "What we think is happening when you're telling your own musical story, [is] you're shutting down impulses that might impede the flow of novel ideas."

Another well-received neuroscience study produced similar findings. University of Western Ontario neuroscientist Daniel Ansari and Aaron Berkowitz, a Harvard graduate student in the department of music, used an fMRI scan like Limb's to study activity in the brain during musical improvisation. Using twelve classically trained pianists in their twenties, Ansari and Berkowitz sought to isolate the creative part of the brain by performing brain scans while the pianists performed four activities. Two general activities had been learned, while the other two were improvised melodies. The pianists did each of these two tasks either with or without a metronome. "We were trying to isolate creativity—or novelty," Berkowitz explained.

Analogous to Limb's findings, Ansari and Berkowitz found that during improvisation, the right-temporoparietal junctions of the pianists' brains were deactivated. Neuroscientists associate this area of the brain with the ability to make judgments, particularly about differences between self and others. The experienced pianists seemed to be able to turn off a judging part of their mind, freeing them up to create novel melodies. According to Berkowitz, brain scans of nonartists do not exhibit a similar pattern, which suggests that experiencing creative processes could help to build certain creative muscles.

Ansari and Berkowitz also found that portions of the brain associated with selecting between two conflicting possibilities lit up during improvisation. This did not surprise them. The brain was generating possibilities and making decisions between choices throughout the improvised melodies. During improvisation, the pianists were making conscious choices and weighing tradeoffs, but freed from the constraints of the part of their brain that makes self versus other judgments, they could concentrate and focus. They were locked in, what psychology researchers might describe as a state of *flow*.

Professor Mihaly Csikszentmihalyi did the pioneering work about the mental state of flow. Csikszentmihalyi had defined flow as: "Being completely involved in an activity for its own sake. The ego falls away. Time flies. Every action, movement, and thought follows inevitably from the previous one, like playing jazz. Your whole being is involved, and you're using your skills to the utmost." We all experience this state of mind from time to time. It's what performers of all kinds, including athletes, musicians, comedians, and dancers, call being *in the zone*, of not being self-conscious. According to Csikszentmihalyi, we are more likely to experience flow when we do work that appeals to our intrinsic interests that's also aligned with our personal strengths.

Attaining a state of flow can be quite rare because there are many barriers to freeing our minds. Csikszentmihalyi identifies negative forms of perfectionism, fear, self-doubt, and self-censoring as primary obstacles to flow. So, the question becomes: How can we counteract these barriers? As Limb's research demonstrated, the area of musicians' brains associated with self-censoring was deactivated during improvisation, so let's dive a bit deeper into improvisational techniques.

There are several major improvisation principles. One is

that you should "accept every offer." So, for example, if two people were performing an improvised skit, Bob might say to Sherry, "I was thinking we could watch *Silence of the Lambs* tonight." To which Sherry would accept that offer by saying something like, "Yes, and we can still have time to watch the *Late Show* afterward." To which Bob might reply, "Yes, and then we can check email!" It's a simplified and somewhat silly example, but the point of accepting every offer is that *nothing* is too silly. Accepting every offer by using "yes . . . and" language, a cornerstone of improvisation, facilitates building up ideas. After all, if Sherry had spurned Bob's initial offer by replying, "That's a stupid movie," Bob would start thinking and censoring himself, shutting down the possibilities that might come. The effect is deadening.

That Bob and Sherry lift one another up relates to another foundation of improvisation: Make your partner look good. Because Bob and Sherry aren't criticizing one another, it creates a positive atmosphere to generate possibilities. Positive energy drives improvisation, and reduces inhibitions and doubts. By making each other look good, it's easier for Bob and Sherry to get in a zone. They can relax and be playful. They're in the moment, and actively listening to each other, so that they can't be planning what they're going to say next. They have to stop thinking and be spontaneous.

Improvisational techniques, therefore, can free us up from the risk aversion and emphasis on rigid procedures that predominate so many workplaces. One company that has made extensive use of these core techniques in its daily operations is Pixar.

Throughout the Pixar creative process, they rely heavily on what they call *plussing*; it is likely the most-used concept around the company. The point of plussing is to build upon and improve ideas without using judgmental language. Creating an atmosphere where ideas are constantly being plussed, while maintaining a sense of humor and playfulness, is a central element of Pixar's magic. The practice of plussing draws upon those core principles from improvisation: accepting every offer and making your partner look good. Rather than criticize an idea in its entirety (even if they don't think it's good), people accept the starting point before suggesting improvements.

To understand how plussing works, imagine that you were an animator working on the movie *Toy Story 3*. The script might call for a scene to last a few seconds (also called a "shot") with the main character, Woody, talking with Buzz Lightyear. The director or supervising animators will assign one or two shots, or a sequence of up to five or seven shots, to animators at a time based on the shot needs and the animator's strengths. Pixar animators produce about one hundred frames per week on average (about four seconds of footage).

After getting a new shot assignment, animators are free to sketch out the scene as they see fit, called "blocking," keeping in mind their deadlines and other constraints such as what comes before or after their shot. Storyboards help animators understand the story flow, including what specific shots come before and after theirs, as well as what feelings the director would like to evoke. (Animators often keep small mirrors on their desks to act out specific facial expressions before producing the animation.) Animators will then take a first pass at their shot. It will be very rough.

At this point, the animator will share her rough sketches and ideas with the film's supervising animator or the director. Pixar's directors are the final decision makers, but not even they will have the final vision for the shot clearly in mind. This is where plussing comes in. Instead of criticizing the sketch or saying "no," the director will build on the starting point by saying something like, "I like Woody's eyes, *and* what if we . . ." Again, notice the use of the word *and* rather than a word that implies a judgment, such as *but*.

So, the director will take the rough material and say something like, "I like Woody's eyes, *and* what if his eyes rolled left?" He'll know what he likes when he sees it, at least directionally, and that's the point of plussing. "You always want to present your ideas in a constructive manner and be respectful of the other animator's feelings," Pixar animator Victor Navone says. "I usually start my suggestions with 'what if' or 'would it be clearer if' [the character] did it this way." As Pete Docter, director of *Monsters Inc.* and *Up*, puts it, "I think everyone [at Pixar] has gotten very good at plussing ideas or changing directions without judging."

Imagine how intimidating it might be to work as an animator at Pixar if plussing weren't the prevailing philosophy. Remember, when animators are deep into working on a film, they submit their draft work each day to a central computer system (regardless of how complete or incomplete), where colleagues can review it. Animation team members will then gather in a conference room each day with the supervising animator and (often) the film's director for dailies. Certain shots are then projected onto a screen and everyone (including the newest animator) is encouraged to share their opinions, ideas, and solutions. Without an atmosphere of offering constructive, nonjudgmental criticism, every day could be an ordeal.

Effective plussing requires that people let go of the need to control every detail. Pete Docter, for example, has had to learn some important nuances about giving feedback to animators. Consider two ways that Docter could give feedback. One is very specific. "You can say, 'Okay, in this scene, on frame number forty-seven, I want his arm reaching across, he's going to grab the glasses case and in seven frames, he's going to move up and hold it above his head,' " he relates. Well, that's not how Docter does it because, again, he doesn't actually know all the specifics in advance. He can't. With literally millions of fine grain considerations and details in each film, there's too much complexity.

The other way to provide feedback is to give general direction and plus ideas in an upbeat manner. Docter demonstrates this by imagining a conversation he might have with an animator about a scene where one character is taunting another. "Okay, he's taunting, you know how when you play with your little brother and you grab the thing and then you go like, 'Yeah? Huh, huh, huh?!' " Docter says, with a playful giggle and glint in his eye as he acts the body language out. "You act it out for them and they get the feeling of, 'Oh, I remember doing that.' Then, it's up to them if it's frame number forty-seven, or even if it's any of the frames. How do we communicate this feeling of taunting?" Docter continues, "If you can use a language that allows them to put in their own specifics, then it becomes much more truthful, they're probably *way* better actors or lighters than I am, so I'm using their talents or their skills to make the movie better and better." The animator walks away, perhaps laughing about Docter's anecdote, and is motivated to produce the shot on her own terms.

Not providing overly specific feedback was a tricky thing for Docter to get used to, but it has become part of Pixar's culture. "There are a lot of different ways to show that a character is uncoordinated or nervous or scared," Docter shares. "As long as that story beat comes across, it's a chance to bring all this talent that these guys have in executing that." Docter's approach goes back to the way John Lasseter role modeled being a director. When Lasseter is in meetings, say, with animators, he will listen to and applaud ideas from everyone, regardless of experience level.

Of course, it's a balance. As ideas become more developed, it's critical to be able to evaluate them and determine their relevance. At the end of the day, after all, Pixar directors get paid to evaluate and connect their ideas with the audience's deep desires and feelings. If the work isn't doing so, they must put their fingers on the problems. Animators at Pixar freely describe how painful it can be to have directors plussing ideas until the smallest details, say a sliver of hair, seem just perfect, but plussing allows for both pointed critique and positive feedback simultaneously, so that even such persistent criticism is not deflating.

This is where the perfectionism research findings relate back to the value of improvisational techniques. Cultivating an environment that allows for playfulness and is positively building, as with plussing, quiets the voice of unhealthy perfectionism and embraces healthy perfectionism.

The research literature is rich with findings about how another aspect of playfulness opens up our inventive juices. If you walk through the corridors at Pixar's headquarters in Emeryville, California, for thirty minutes, you will almost certainly hear laughter. "Brahhaaaa!" the laughs chorused as four people walked through the company's large central atrium. It turned out to be Bob Petersen, a senior member of Pixar's story team, with three colleagues. Although the specific dialogue was impossible to decipher, Petersen was reeling off one line after another, and his (younger) colleagues literally had beet-red cheeks. One was on the verge of tears. They were in hysterics, something that few workplaces would accept, an interesting contrast with dominant buttoned-up professional norms, parodied exquisitely in the movie *Office Space* or television show *The Office*. Straitlaced. Uncontroversial. Professional. Certainly not playful. Humor is so prominent at Pixar that it was worthy of deeper investigation.

A host of studies indicates that humor creates positive group effects. Many focus on how humor can increase cohesiveness and act as a lubricant to facilitate more efficient communications, like Bob Petersen's story team. Researchers have developed a general view that effective humor can increase the quantity and quality of group communications. One reason for that is that humor has also been demonstrated to increase trust. In a widely cited study, Professor William Hampes examined the relationship between humor and trust among eighty-nine college undergraduates ranging in age from sixteen to fifty-four and found a significant correlation. The people who scored high on a test that measured sense of humor for social purposes, coping humor, and appreciated humor and humorous people were considered more trustworthy.

In order to produce positive mental effects, however, researchers Eric Romero and Anthony Pescosolido found that humor first must be considered funny to the people involved, not seen as demeaning, derogatory, or put-downs. That finding is consistent with the underlying improvisation rationale for accepting every offer and making your partner look good. Successful group humor, Romero and Pescosolido argued, based on a broad assessment of humor research, should affirm group identities in terms of: who we are, what we are doing, and how we do things.

Group leaders set the tone. Much like John Lasseter's or Bob Petersen's approach at Pixar, successful humor breaks down the power structures that tend to inhibit tighter social bonds and interactions. This is precisely the type of environment Pixar seeks to create. They have established that, at Pixar, hierarchy and positional status are of less relevance than at most companies. The dominant hierarchical work environment supports the fallacy that the most experienced or senior person in the group will have the answers. People around Google and other corners of Silicon Valley often refer to this as the *HiPPO* phenomenon. That is, the highest paid person's opinion (HiPPO) usually dominates how people make decisions inside most organizations. People look to the HiPPO to make decisions. People equate status and money with intelligence and insight, when often there's little correlation.

Catmull, Lasseter, and Docter will freely admit that, as the most experienced people at Pixar, they don't have all the answers. Everyone at Pixar knows this. As Silicon Valley blogger Chris Yeh says, "Pixar should be commended for being the anti-HiPPOs." While Lasseter can put on his marketing and executive hat with other corporate executives (say at Disney), when it comes to the idea-generation phase, he is like a big kid in many ways, and he constantly uses playful humor to set the tone.

This is an important point. A playful, lighthearted, and humorous environment is especially helpful when ideas are incubating and newly hatched, the phase when they are most vulnerable to being snuffed out or even expressed because of being judged or self-censored. The imagined possibilities become the basis for little bets, just as comedians improvise to develop new material. Plussing then forms the basis by which to build ideas toward perfection. However, as John Lasseter expresses his perfectionism, "We don't actually finish our films, we release them."

CHAPTER 5

Problems Are
the New Solutions

When Frank Gehry speaks, he likes to draw. Hunched over a yellow legal pad with a black pen, he sketches a wiggling, expansive cloud. An outsider might assume that Disney Concert Hall's parabolic metallic structure grew out of a chaotic creative process. But no. "I'm misunderstood. They think I'm doing this," he says, pointing to the cloud, "but if I was, I wouldn't be here today." He marks four dots then connects them to form a square box inside the cloud. "The realities are these constraints," he says, staring intently with his blue eyes, his pen tip resting inside the square. "Nobody realizes this." Gehry then sets his pen down and begins to explain.

Instrumental in this process was the way in which Gehry and his team made use of the constraints imposed upon them for the project. On a typical project, the constraints, what Gehry also calls "guard rails," that define the scope of Gehry's figurative box will include a budget, timeframe, materials, political or regulatory rules, and the nature of the building site itself. Those constraints not only help Gehry Partners to bound, focus, and measure their progress, they help begin and evolve the design. As Google's Marissa Mayer has put it, "Constraints shape and focus problems and provide clear challenges to overcome." Mayer's description is elegant. As we'll see, productively creative people use constraints to limit their focus and isolate a set of problems that need to be solved. Gehry's ideas can be outlandish, but they must happen within the box.

Without constraints, Gehry feels lost. He was once asked to design a house without them. "I had a horrible time with it," he shared. "I had to look in the mirror a lot. Who am I? Why am I doing this? What is this all about?" The possibilities were limitless. The owner eventually gave Gehry an Oscar Wilde quote as guidance. "I can't remember the quote, but it was in essence that everything didn't have to be relevant, that you could make a folly, and that there was some value in that," Gehry recalled. "I think we turn those constraints into action."

A great case in point of how a particular constraint can lead Gehry's way was the standards set for the acoustics of Disney Hall. The hall, a towering and expansive metallic structure resembling a giant ship with its sails unfurled in the wind, opened in downtown Los Angeles in 2003. The building is not without its critics, but a 2006 *US News & World Report* article described its effect on the downtown:

> Disney Hall, with its soaring, steel surfaces and breathtaking mix of beauty, grace, and optimism, is downtown L.A.'s "it" building. Completed in 2003, it is the envy of orchestras around the world and has given L.A. the kind of cultural credibility that had eluded it for years. It has also become the focal point of a nearly $2 billion downtown renaissance.

Gehry's achievement with Disney Hall is thrown into stark relief by comparison to the building directly across the street: the Dorothy Chandler Pavilion, a large, 1960s-era cement building surrounded by pillars modeled after Greek columns. With 3,200 seats, the large performance theater played host to the Academy Awards from 1969 to 1987 and again from 1990 to 1994. Welton Becket, the architect who designed Chandler Pavilion, unabashedly modeled the building on Lincoln Center in New York. Becket even put the Chandler on a raised podium, like Lincoln Center, which was built that way on the theory that it would lift the building above the impoverished surrounding neighborhood. It's easy for passersby to miss the Chandler. No one misses the dramatic presence of Disney Hall.

Contrasting Disney Hall with the Chandler Pavilion, the buildings illustrate two diametrically different approaches to doing something new. Welton Becket based the design for the Chandler on existing knowledge and a known solution: Lincoln Center. It's a common phenomenon. Gehry's design, by contrast, is distinctively original, and what's particularly insightful about that originality is the approach Gehry uses to achieve it.

Disney Hall did not appear to Gehry as a fully developed image, or a singular idea. It emerged through a process of little bets through which Gehry and his team worked within constraints to frame and identify thousands of problems. Gehry's firm won the competition to design Disney Hall through a blind selection process and an important factor in the selection was that Lillian Disney, Walt Disney's widow, especially liked the way the gardens were portrayed in Gehry's initial designs. The hall looks completely different today. Gehry's team worked through a host of issues before the final design emerged, from creating premium acoustics to a number of urban-planning challenges. Along the way, they received feedback and guidance from the Disney family, the Los Angeles Philharmonic, and many others. Gehry and his team would, in fact, create eighty-two prototype models, working closely with the planning committee, until they arrived at the final form of the hall. "I didn't gerrymander the design," Gehry says, "It grew out of the project." Put another way, if the Chandler Pavilion design came primarily from one idea (Lincoln Center), the Disney Hall design evolved from thousands, if not millions, of small discoveries.

The planning committee wanted the acoustics to rival the best in the world, but there was no preordained manner that was to be achieved. Gehry himself had a particular desire to create intimate acoustics. He imagined the hall would be a "living room for the city," a relaxing place where people could enjoy great music. And he wanted the audience to have, as he puts it, a "kind of magical experience." He believed that would happen when a relationship developed between the performers and the audience, and that the right acoustics would be central to making that happen.

To illustrate the role that premium acoustics played in developing the conception for the overall design, Gehry returns to his notepad and outlines the inside of the hall. He sketches a space to represent the performance area, surrounded by the audience. After drawing small circles to represent orchestra members, he connects them together with small lines. His voice enlivens and he says, "They [people in the orchestra] play better when they can hear each other, so you make that original sound perfect."

He then begins to sketch how that idea connects to the audience experience. Drawing small dots to represent audience members, he moves his hand back and forth between the orchestra and audience. "The audience feels the orchestra playing better, and [responds]." He then draws circles around the two groups to indicate positively reinforcing feedback between the audience and performers. "The orchestra feels that response," he says. Gehry nearly punctures the paper as he moves his pen back and forth between the small circles representing the audience and the performers.

To attain the highest acoustical standards, Gehry would get an invaluable partner in Yasuhisa Toyota, the chief acoustician for Disney Hall. Toyota was part of Nagata Acoustics, a small Japanese consulting firm specializing in developing performance-hall acoustics. Gehry worked with him and his team to experiment with a host of ideas for audio enhancement through dozens of prototype models. They considered a wide range of possibilities for the wall paneling, seating configuration and arrangements, and the ceiling height. As they worked with these possibilities, the performance hall design began to take its distinctive shape and feel.

An important early decision was to discard the standard shoebox concert hall design. According to this design, the orchestra sits on a raised stage at one end of the hall. Gehry, in collaboration with the planning committee, opted instead for a vineyard configuration, in which the audience surrounds the orchestra in terraced seating, where seats rise in all four directions from the central stage. Each seat has a clear line of sight to the stage. This arrangement was cozy, much like theater in the round, and would both help to create the intimate experience Gehry was looking for and improve the acoustics by increasing the area via which the sound would be reflected, a central way to amplify sound and envelop listeners.

Yasuhisa Toyota and Gehry then worked within these parameters to enhance the sound reflection, a crucial component of good acoustics. The most important sound reflections come soon after the direct sound, the ones that bounce off the performance hall's side walls surrounding the orchestra. This guided a number of decisions, including that the seats would be configured in terraced style. The vineyard seating configuration also emphasizes receiving lateral sound reflections from sidewall panels. The room was then lined with free-standing walls and wood paneled partitions were placed in the audience, which both enhanced the acoustics and created a natural atmosphere and feeling. Meanwhile, the ceiling height was set at fifteen-and-a-half meters, driven by extended reverberation needs: A low ceiling could reflect frequencies effectively from above. They also used an array of concave curves (bulging inward, toward the hall) whenever possible, such as on the ceiling or the walls, another acoustic technique known to enhance sound. These decisions then influenced the design for the rest of the building, since Gehry would design the exterior around the inner cavity of the building, including the auditorium and a small side recital hall. According to Gehry, "The entire building was designed from the inside out."

They measured their progress through eighty-two models at one-tenth scale. The way that acoustics get tested in models is by scaling sound waves to the size of the model. Toyota described how the process works. "We emit sounds at ten times their normal frequency, record them at ten times their regular speed, then play them back ten times slower. This will accurately represent sound within the model."

Ultimately, they would obtain a reverberation time of 2.2 seconds in an unoccupied hall and 2.0 seconds in an occupied one, which is considered optimal for orchestra music. Once the 2,265-seat auditorium was completed, the Los Angeles Philharmonic Orchestra had four months to acclimate to their new home. Their response was wildly enthusiastic. "The beautiful thing about the hall is the realism of the sound," conductor Esa-Pekka Salonen said in an interview with PBS. The Philharmonic's previous home had been across the street, at Chandler Pavilion. Disney Hall's acoustics would allow Salonen to perform a wider range of music, including Schoenberg's *Guerrelieder*. "I love the new hall, truly love it," Salonen gushed. "It's not only that ticket sales have skyrocketed, it's the fact that people in Los Angeles, and outside Los Angeles as well, can take on a whole new awareness of what music can add to the quality of life."

Throughout building design process, Gehry's team constantly checks a project's progress against its constraints. One way they do so is by using an electronic pen to scan each model into a computer using proprietary software called Digital Project. Someone does this by hand. The software, originally developed for aerospace companies, then maps and documents the design. It calculates the work in progress at scale against project constraints, including the floor area, volume, and surface area of a building. And, Gehry makes a point of noting, it's accurate up to seven decimal places.

The fact that working with constraints is so helpful in providing structure and guides doesn't mean that it's easy; it can be excruciating. On Gehry's team, if a building model exceeds its parameters after it gets scanned into the computer, Gehry says his colleagues might approach him with disappointed, long-faced expressions. "I say, 'God, the design looks good but you've got to take ten percent of this away.'" This is instrumental in pushing them to refine the design. Architectural plans can then be generated with specifications for contractors, down to details as to where to place titanium panels or stone blocks. And so, constraints both help Gehry to decide what to do as well as what not to do.

Being able to effectively use constraints takes some doing. With some endeavors, such as architecture, constraints are clearly imposed from the outside. At other times, the possibilities seem limitless, such as the blank-page problem. In situations like these, using self-imposed constraints is a powerful technique. The key is to take a larger project or goal and break it down into smaller problems to be solved, constraining the scope of work to solving a key problem, and then another key problem.

This strategy, of breaking a project down into discrete, relatively small problems to be resolved, is what Bing Gordon, a cofounder and the former chief creative officer of the video game company Electronic Arts, calls *smallifying*. Now a partner at the venture capital firm Kleiner Perkins, Gordon has deep experience leading and working with software development teams. He's also currently on the board of directors of Amazon and Zynga. At Electronic Arts, Gordon found that when software teams worked on longer-term projects, they were inefficient and took unnecessary paths. However, when job tasks were broken down into particular problems to be solved, which were manageable and could be tackled within one or two weeks, developers were more creative and effective.

This practice of smallifying problems is a common one in Silicon Valley these days, related to what executives call one of the most important recent ideas in the software industry: agile software development. Unveiled in 2001, the founders of agile development, including Kent Beck, Alistair Cockburn, and Jeff Sutherland and fourteen other software developers, believed that software development projects should be broken into small pieces, prioritized, completed, and released based on user needs. They emphasized using small collaborative teams to respond to change over determined processes or plans, and believed that working software was the best measure of progress.

Interestingly, the founders of one line of agile development essentially took the core elements for their approach from the Japanese manufacturing playbook. Jeff Sutherland, a founder of the scrum method, says they went so far as to take that term from a 1986 *Harvard Business Review* article. In that article, the authors Hirotaka Takeuchi and Ikujiro Nonaka described best practices in new product development at places like Honda, Canon, and Fuji. As Sutherland recalls, "We looked at the way they set up their teams and we set up ours in *exactly* the same way."

Takeuchi and Nonaka compared the way Japanese product development teams organized themselves with the way a rugby team might drive down the field in a scrum formation, passing the ball back and forth to the right person for each moment of play. Rugby teams make creative decisions according to the challenge just before them, from which the specific path downfield emerges. Likewise, the Japanese teams were crossfunctional, had autonomy largely unobstructed by top management, would self organize, and would learn what to do as they proceeded. Rather than use detailed planning processes and divvy up the job tasks, like the ones General Motors had used to develop new products, new venture teams at Honda combined designers, engineers, production, and sales; the teams would stay intact from beginning to end. The team's goal was to achieve greater speed and flexibility, while management imposed constraints, what the authors called "subtle controls," such as project checkpoints. Takeuchi and Nonaka likened this approach to the way rugby teams seek to draw upon the particular talents of each team member at just the right moment.

By contrast, software traditionally is developed in a way in which the solution is planned, designed, and detailed before the project begins. This is often known as the "waterfall method." So, if Microsoft wants to launch a new version of Windows using waterfall, problems are identified and combined with designs and solutions up front. Rather than rely on small teams to identify problems and solutions, waterfall processes are managed in a top-down manner, whereby senior people map out and control the project. It's called "waterfall" because the process begins with the program's requirements then flows down to its design, before moving to the implementation, testing, and installation. Requirements documents often run one hundred pages long and job tasks are listed in phase-by-phase Gantt charts, which map specific project tasks and timelines in bar charts.

In fact, the waterfall standard grew largely out of the United States' Department of Defense (DoD). In the 1980s, the Defense department funded roughly 60 percent of all software development projects and mandated that its contractors use waterfall methods. Given the DoD's influence, the rest of the software development industry essentially followed suit.

Although the waterfall method has its virtues, among them visibility and control over the process (since the project schedule is mapped out in Gantt charts), there are several major flaws. One is that managers try to anticipate every conceivable software feature users might need at the outset. As Steve Jobs is known to say, "People don't know what they want if they haven't seen it." Not surprisingly, many features created through waterfall methods are never used. Another flaw is that by the time a company like Microsoft, say, finishes a one-

or two-year software project, the world may have changed. The problems are different. The premium that the waterfall approach places on up-front planning so that glitches in the requirements or design don't disrupt the project after months (or years) of work have become an ever bigger problem as the Internet has increased the pace of technology change. Factors like these have helped fuel the increasing popularity of agile development.

Inherent to agile development is to focus on smallified pieces of work and narrowly defined problems. However, the problems to be solved become better known throughout the process, rather than at the outset. This involves something that creativity research has shown to be a central aide to any creative process: the ability to actively seek out problems, just as Gehry does using the constraints he's under, such as to identify ways to enhance acoustics. Psychologists Jacob Getzels and Mihaly Csikszentmihalyi conducted a seminal study in the 1970s that highlighted the importance of problem finding to creative work.

In a study of thirty-five artists, Getzels and Csikszentmihalyi found that the most creative in their sample were more open to experimentation and to reformulating their ideas for projects than their less creative counterparts. The artists were shown twenty-seven objects, such as cups or trash bins, and were asked to use some of the objects to create a drawing. Problem finders looked at more objects and selected more complicated ones to draw than their counterparts. Finders then explored more possibilities and were willing to switch direction with their drawings when new opportunities presented themselves. Gehry's approach illustrates problem finding. The less creative artists, on the other hand, immediately jumped to drawing objects, leading the researchers to call them "problem solvers." A panel of independent judges found the problem finders' work markedly more creative than the problem solvers' work. In a follow-up study completed eighteen years later, this one expanded to also include scientists, the researchers found that the work of active problem finders was more critically acclaimed as determined by their peers and other expert judges.

Whereas one of the main reasons the waterfall method is criticized is that it leaves little room to reformulate problems, the agile method of seeking out problems throughout the development process is similar to the approach followed by HP in its more innovative days. Similar to the way HP's staff found hosts of customer problems, including for its first computer, the agile process begins when people working in marketing or sales roles for a company identify customer problems or needs. So, let's say the company makes software to support sales teams. The customer need might be to be able to link their email contact files with the sales software system, so that users don't have to copy and paste files one by one. The product manager at the software company aggregates and prioritizes a running list of these requests in an Excel spreadsheet.

Every week or two, the product manager conducts a meeting with the software development and testing team to discuss and divvy up the workload. The teams are typically composed of six to seven people. Her first order of business is to estimate how much time each piece of work will take. She begins with the highest priority item for that two-week period; let's say it's a module to transfer email contact files into the software. People briefly discuss what the job will require, then hold up numerical cards indicating the number of hours or days they think it will take. They'll typically roughly agree about how much time each task will take, often a few days or a week. If there's an outlier or two, they might have a short discussion and take another vote. They'll work through the list of priorities like this until they've maximized the available developer time for the next two weeks. Meeting adjourned, they are off to their sprint.

Once they finish and test the piece of software to transfer email contact files, for example, the feature will be included in an upcoming release.

Not only does the smallifying process facilitate the more efficient development of code, but it also promotes faster learning. As any user of Adobe, Apple's iTunes, or Microsoft Office knows, new software releases occur far more frequently than in the past. That's in large part because once a new feature is released the company can learn how well it's solving user problems or needs. In the case above, for example, product managers would analyze usage data in order to determine if people were transferring their email contact files as anticipated. The product managers might quickly find that many users want to make new entries into their contact files in multiple places, such as their email and their phones. If that appears to be an important enough user need or problem, the product manager will prioritize developing code to address it in her Excel spreadsheet. She will have found a new problem.

To see how smallifying can be instrumental in terms of developing a new business, consider the way that Andre Vanier and his business partner, Mike Slemmer, developed their free 411 online information service called 1-800-411-SAVE. Vanier is a former McKinsey Consultant where he worked with some of America's largest organizations before being pulled away by an entrepreneurial fervor following graduate school. He and Slemmer had different views at first about how they should go about writing the code for the company. Vanier envisioned what he considered to be the correct approach: develop software that would right from the beginning be able to support the millions of users they hoped to eventually bring to the service. Slemmer, however, had already cofounded two technology companies and thought they should instead build the software more incrementally, in stages that were appropriate to the growth of users.

Slemmer could guarantee Vanier that when they got to ten thousand users, they would realize that many of their assumptions about the problems they were trying to solve, established with their first ten test users, were completely wrong. And when they get to one million users, they would almost certainly have to rip up and rewrite large sections of the software code because of the new insights they would have learned. It would be the same story at ten million. So, Slemmer asked, did Vanier really want to try to answer all those questions before they had a single user? "We took his approach," Vanier reflects. Although they competed against substantially larger, better-resourced companies, such as 1-800-FREE-411, they were consistently first to identify new features and services such as driving directions and integrated web-phone promotional offers.

Note that one of the great benefits of the agile approach is that it is also a good method for failing fast. As Vanier explains, if he can launch ten features in the same time it takes a competitor to launch one, he'll have ten times the amount of experience to draw from in figuring out what has failed the test of customer acceptance and what has succeeded.

Agile development is not without its limitations, such as when large teams must be coordinated, but well-run agile teams have regularly achieved higher productivity and quality than the waterfall method. This helps explain why established companies like Intuit, Yahoo!, and Salesforce.com have followed nimble startups, like Andre Vanier's, toward agile methods.

The imposition of constraints is a powerful technique across a wide range of endeavors. It was, to use another example, central to the turnaround in the strategy in the Iraq war. At the time that U.S. Army Brigadier General H. R. McMaster was brought to Iraq in 2004, the war had reached a crucial turning point. During 2003 and 2004, the Pentagon strategy in Iraq was known as "kill-and-capture," whereby the U.S. military would raid Iraqi cities seeking to eliminate insurgents. "For several years, we fought a war in Iraq that was often counterproductive," military author Thomas Ricks described it. "We had our troops in big bases; they called them FOBs, Forward Operating Bases. And they would go out in vehicles: Humvees, Bradleys, and tanks, and do patrols [there were the raids] and then go back to their bases. They really didn't have a feel for the population in a lot of places." They weren't solving the right problems.

McMaster advocated for a different approach. A passionate, lifelong military man, McMaster is now in his mid forties. In person, the laser-focused intensity and rigid scowl he generally wears in official Army photos gives way to a gregarious nature. A hero of the first Gulf War, McMaster attended Valley Forge Military Academy and West Point and has lived and breathed the military since, both on the battlefield and as a PhD in military history. By the Iraq war, he had risen to become one of the Army's top counterinsurgency specialists and strategic thinkers. In being brought in to take charge of operations in the city of Tal Afar, he would get the chance to prove his theories in the heat of battle.

Perched roughly twenty-five miles from the Syrian border, Tal Afar had become a gruesome place. By late 2004, a population of roughly two hundred fifty thousand had endured numerous failed attempts by American forces to quell the insurgents who had wreaked havoc on the city. Al-Qaeda had established significant operations there as its training base for Iraq, which included a beheading cell and preparation ground for suicide bombers. The city buildings were crumbling, the mud streets were deeply grated by armored vehicle tracks, and the population had largely gone into hiding, nervously peering out from their shutters.

Raiding was the strategy used in Tal Afar during 2004 by the small, five-thousand-soldier Army Stryker brigade. According to McMaster, they fought valiantly but the insurgents temporarily slid out of Tal Afar into surrounding areas. "There weren't enough forces to do anything but raid to disrupt the enemy," he says. Complicating matters, the Stryker mission, poorly dubbed "Black Typhoon," fueled a sophisticated insurgent propaganda campaign (mostly al-Qaeda operatives) that portrayed American forces as attacking the Tal Afar people. Many locals believed it. When the cavalry arrived in the spring of 2005, jihadists again largely controlled the city.

When then-Colonel H. R. McMaster and the 3rd Cavalry arrived on the ground near Tal Afar in the spring of 2005, they couldn't plan farther than they could see. Uncertainty reigned. Blurry lines between friend and foe greatly complicated American operations, and the fear of the local population was pulling people toward the insurgency who might otherwise support a legitimate government.

McMaster was given a mandate—to secure and hold Tal Afar—but rather than make a bold offensive move, he constrained his forces' actions. They spent the first thirty days performing focused area reconnaissance, acting as problem finders. Patrols extended west along the Syrian border and south toward the Euphrates river. "We basically went into the areas that were completely unknown to us," he says. They used this reconnaissance to identify and frame discrete problems to tackle. One of these was the need to develop better relationships with local tribal leaders to understand the local power structure. As we've already seen, to facilitate this, they set up several patrol bases within Tal Afar and lived within the population, so that they could keep their ears low to the ground and experience the local conditions, such as a lack of electricity. Another problem they identified, taking advice from Iraqis, was how insurgents moved into and out of the city, smuggling supplies, people, and money, through an array of porous points. Again, the solution was to ring Tal Afar with a nine-foot-tall dirt berm that established only three points of entry and exit, which they made into checkpoints to monitor and control the flow of goods and people into and out of the city.

Another key problem identified was the safe houses that were harboring insurgents and their weapons. On reconnaissance missions and through intelligence collection, McMaster's forces identified these safe houses and moved on them one by one. They were methodically constraining their activities around one smallified problem after another.

McMaster then identified a larger problem to tackle, using what his troops had learned from their thirty-day period of reconnaissance activities. The nearby town of Biaj, with a population of just fifteen thousand, had been identified as a hub of al-Qaeda planning and financing, a base for the smuggling of oil, sheep, and cigarettes. McMaster trained his sights on taking control of the town. By that time, his forces had the insight to know exactly where to go and what to do. A cavalry squadron, an Iraqi Army battalion, and the exiled city police force converged on the city from the south and the west. Within a day, they captured nineteen insurgents, began building a base inside the city to house the Iraqi Army battalion, and reinstalled the city police and government. "This was the first 'clear and hold,' " McMaster recalled in an interview, which caught the attention of senior State Department and defense officials. The successful operation in Biaj "was sort of a rehearsal, on a very small scale [for Tal Afar]," McMaster says.

Even after the important success, though, McMaster constrained his action. The reconnaissance missions uncovered that al-Qaeda housed its six-hundred-person Battalion of One True God on the eastern side of the city, and that the area was its training base for all of Iraq. The safe haven included a mortar school, an IED school, a sniper school, a course on kidnapping and murder, and an information operations cell. McMaster waited four months to launch an attack, however, to allow for the steps he had taken to weaken the insurgents' support structure to take effect. When he gave the go-ahead, his forces did still experience heavy fighting, but the combined American and Iraqi forces steadily retook control of the city. By 2006, a delicate peace formed that would improve and endure.

Back in Washington, this successful clear-hold-and-build in Tal Afar contributed to a significant shift in U.S. strategy. Emulating McMaster's Tal Afar approach, Colonel Sean Mac-Farland secured the city of Ramadi during 2006. The news stunned observers. Ramadi had had the highest attack levels in Iraq. A tipping point had arrived and, following high-level strategic discussions, General David Petraeus, the army's leading counterinsurgency expert, was ordered to take command in Iraq during early 2007 to implement the strategy on the large scale.

Given the fear or indecision we often confront when attempting to unleash our creativity, the practice of rigorously smallifying problems is liberating. At the same time, while some externally imposed constraints can be onerous, many can be enormously helpful starting points. This is the great irony about constraints. And if we can delineate the job before us into discrete problems to solve, as General McMaster, agile developers, and Gehry do by taking a proactive approach to problem finding, we are more likely to discover unique possibilities.

CHAPTER 6

Questions Are
the New Answers

One of the best ways to identify creative insights and develop ideas is to throw out the theory and experience things first-hand. After all, fresh problems, ideas, needs, and desires aren't obvious; they're hidden beneath the surface. We can't even know what questions to ask until we reach beyond what is already known through a true process of discovery: carefully exploring, observing, and listening to uncover what is hidden from the naked eye from the bottom up. In doing so, we must go deep, we must go wide, and we must be focused. Let's take each in turn.

David Galenson's examination of prominent creators' work processes has illuminated the enormous value of immersion in unfamiliar terrain. Galenson has one foot firmly planted in two parallel universes. He's a tenured professor of economics at the University of Chicago, yet his core passion (and body of research) is examining how artists and creators work. He has spent years chronicling the creative processes and methods prominent creators use, and one of his favorite examples of the importance of immersion is Muhammad Yunus, the founder of the Grameen Bank, the lender responsible for launching the microfinance industry, and recipient of the 2006 Nobel Peace Prize.

In 1974, Yunus was an economics professor at Chittagong University in Bangladesh. That year, a severe famine ravaged Bangladesh sending starving, skeletonlike people from the countryside into cities in search of food. They started showing up in railway stations and bus stations, Yunus recalled in his autobiography, *Banker to the Poor*. Soon the trickle became a flood. People were collapsing in the streets by the thousands, slowly dying, without cries or protests. Some sat so still, no one could tell whether they were alive or dead. Research institutions gathered statistics about the causes of the sudden migration, but soon the number of dead bodies exceeded the means to collect and bury them.

Yunus began to dread his own lectures. "What good were all my complex theories when people were dying of starvation on the sidewalks and porches outside my lecture hall?" he asked himself. "Nothing in the economic theories I taught reflected the life around me." It was Yunus's opinion that "Economists spend their talents detailing the processes for development and prosperity, but rarely reflect the origin and development of poverty and hunger." So he decided to do something quite unconventional, as Yunus the economist became Yunus the anthropologist.

Leaping forward two years, a woman named Sufiya Begum squatted barefoot outside the hut where she lived, its mud walls crumbling and thatched roof pockmarked with holes. Sufiya lived in one of the poorest neighborhoods of Jobra, a small village not far from Chittagong where Yunus taught. Her hands moved quickly around a half-completed bamboo stool that she held between her knees. Sufiya's fingers were severely callused, her fingernails blackened by grime. She was completely engaged by her work. Hearing the greeting of Yunus's colleague, Professor H. I. Latifee, Sufiya dropped the bamboo and sprang to her feet to run inside. "Don't be frightened," Latifee called out in her dialect. "We are not strangers. We teach up at the university . . . We want to ask you a few questions, that is all." But Sufiya hid inside so they could not see her. "There's nobody home," she responded in a quiet voice, meaning that no men were home. (Women in Bangladesh are not supposed to speak with men other than close family members.)

It was here, in the village of Jobra, where Yunus absorbed himself in the lives of some of Bangladesh's poorest people, seeking to understand poverty from what he called *the worm's-eye view.* "When you hold the world in your palm and inspect it only from a bird's-eye view, you tend to become arrogant—you do not realize that things get blurred when seen from an enormous distance," Yunus wrote. He spent time with women who separated rice from straw with their bare feet ten hours per day. He toiled with farmers in the fields to try to help them improve their irrigation systems and crop yields. And he went home to home (or, hut to hut) to understand how people like Sufiya made their living. The insights he learned, from people like Sufiya, informed his experiments. "I tried a great number of things," Yunus wrote. "Some worked. Others did not." Helping a small group of farmers improve their crop yields, for example, only went so far. The impact was relatively small.

As Sufiya hid inside her hut, her naked children ran around the front yard while chickens scrounged for food. Neighbors glared out on the scene. Seeking to comfort Sufiya, Yunus picked up one of her children and held him for a moment saying, "He is very beautiful, this one," until the child began crying and kicked free to race to his mother. Cautiously, Sufiya came to the doorway, holding the baby.

"What is your name?" Yunus asked.

"Sufiya Begum."

"How old are you?"

"Twenty-one."

"Do you own this bamboo?"

"Yes."

"How do you get it?" Yunus continued.

"I buy it," she replied.

"How much does the bamboo cost you?"

"Five taka." (About twenty-two cents at the time)

"Do you have five taka?"

"No, I borrow it from paikars."

"The middlemen?" Yunus asked. "What is your arrangement with them?"

"I must sell my bamboo stools back to them at the end of the day as repayment for my loan," she replied.

"How much do you sell a stool for?"

"Five taka and fifty poysha."

"So you make fifty poysha profit?" Yunus continued. (That was a profit of two cents.)

Sufiya nodded.

"And could you borrow the cash from the moneylender and buy your own raw material?"

"Yes, but the moneylender would demand a lot," she replied. "People who deal with them only get poorer."

"How much does the moneylender charge?" Yunus inquired.

"It depends. Sometimes he charges ten percent [interest] per week. But I have one neighbor who is paying ten percent per day." Imagine that.

"And that is all you earn from making these beautiful bamboo stools, fifty poysha?" Yunus asked.

"Yes," Sufiya replied as she squatted again and started moving her hands quickly around the bamboo stool.

Yunus felt shocked. He especially could not believe that Sufiya earned just two cents per day. "In my university courses, I theorized about sums in the millions of dollars, but here before my eyes the problems of life and death were posed in terms of pennies," he recounted. "Something was wrong. Why did my university courses not reflect the reality of Sufiya's life? I was angry, angry at myself, angry at my economics department and the thousands of intelligent professors who had not tried to address this problem and solve it." Nothing foreseeable would break the cycle of poverty for Sufiya, or for her children. "I had never heard anyone suffering for the lack of *twenty-two cents*," Yunus lamented.

Yunus went back to his house where he and Professor Latifee took a walk through the garden in the late afternoon heat. "I was trying to see Sufiya's problem from her point of view," Yunus recalled. "She suffered because the cost of bamboo was five taka." Sufiya could not afford to buy raw materials for the bamboo stools and she could not get a conventional loan since she did not have collateral. The middlemen allowed her just enough profit to survive from day to day. Sufiya lived as a bonded laborer, essentially enslaved.

The next day, Yunus asked one of his students to compile a list of people in Jobra who, like Sufiya, were dependent upon middlemen. The list came to forty-two people. They needed a combined total of less than twenty-seven dollars to finance their work. "My god, my god. All this misery in all these families and all for the lack of twenty-seven dollars!" Yunus exclaimed. His student stood silently, not saying a word. What kept Sufiya in poverty wasn't a lack of effort. It was a lack of formal credit that allowed middlemen to fill the gap. By immersing himself in Sufiya's life, Yunus had discovered a core problem that economists had overlooked.

Yunus never intended to be a moneylender. Yet, after making the first twenty-seven-dollar loan personally, he secured the capital necessary to start the Grameen Bank in 1977. Grameen would provide very poor, self-employed people, 96 percent of whom would be women, with tiny loans. Consistent with Saras Sarasvathy's findings about the entrepreneurial process, Yunus would have to act with determination to generate support and allies, including to overcome deep skepticism within the Indian banking community that India's poorest were creditworthy. But, over the coming years, Grameen would loan over $6.5 billion, while maintaining repayment rates consistently above 98 percent. The practice became known as "microlending" or "microfinance," and would become a global phenomenon. "All I really wanted to do was solve an immediate problem," he said. As Yunus described in a speech years later, "At the beginning, you had no idea that something like this [microlending] would emerge, but it is so clear, so transparent, you don't need to be a smart researcher to go find it."

The insights and ideas that were obvious to Yunus the anthropologist had been hidden from Yunus the economist. The difference: by absorbing poverty from the worm's-eye view, asking lots of questions, and being open to changing his assumptions, he could understand what he could not from a bird's-eye view. He could *feel* Sufiya's poverty. And it was here, in the marrow of poverty, where Yunus discovered the insights, ideas, and passion to formulate his breakthrough idea. The abstractions were gone. As Steve Blank, a cofounder of the software company E.piphany, who teaches entrepreneurship at Berkeley's Haas School of Business and who routinely challenges entrepreneurs to get out into the world to challenge their own assumptions, says, "No facts exist inside the building, only opinions." As a former marketer, Blank's point is that people won't know what problems they are actually solving for customers if they always stay in their cubicles.

Consider the implications for a moment, using army strategy as a lens. Counterinsurgency operators submerge within their battle context in order to understand the local situation. "You gotta come in with your ears open," H. R. McMaster told George Packer inside Tal Afar during 2006, "You can't come in and start talking. You have to really *listen* to people." Using a more anthropological approach to warfare naturally requires a different type of training than standard army fare. So, before their deployment to Iraq, Colonel McMaster and his officers improvised an entirely new training program at Fort Carson, Colorado. Packer, reporting for the *New Yorker*, described the scene:

> Instead of preparing for tank battles, the regiment bought dozens of Arab dishdashas, which the Americans call "man dresses," and acted out a variety of realistic scenarios, with soldiers and Arab-Americans playing the role of Iraqis . . . Pictures of Shiite saints and politicians were hung on the walls of a house, and soldiers were asked to draw conclusions about the occupants. Soldiers searching the house were given the information they wanted only after they had sat down with the occupants three or four times, accepted tea, and asked the right questions. Soldiers filmed the scenarios and, afterward, analyzed body language and conversational tone. McMaster ordered his soldiers never to swear in front of Iraqis or call them "hajjis" in a derogatory way (this war's

version of "gook"). Some were selected to take three-week courses in Arabic language and culture; hundreds of copies of "The Modern History of Iraq," by Phebe Marr, were shipped to Fort Carson; and McMaster drew up a counterinsurgency reading list that included classic works such as T. E. Lawrence's "Seven Pillars of Wisdom," together with "Learning to Eat Soup with a Knife," a recent study by Lieutenant Colonel John Nagl, a veteran of the Iraq war.

Call it social, cultural, and political immersion. The cavalry needed to soak up Tal Afar from the worm's eye view to understand all that they could not from the bird's-eye view. "When we first got here, we made a lot of mistakes," McMaster shared. "We were like a blind man, trying to do the right thing but breaking a lot of things." So, for example, their initial efforts to recruit a police force yielded just three volunteers. Under the new approach, Lieutenant Colonel Chris Hickey spent forty to fifty hours per week building relationships with local tribal leaders and working to understand the local problems. Hickey would go house to house for tea with residents including those who had ties to the insurgents. Fear and distrust ran deep. Believing the propaganda campaigns and fearing for his life, even the Tal Afar Mayor Najim Abdullah alJabouri had considered joining the insurgency.

Critically, Hickey and a squadron of one thousand American troops actually lived in the city. It was a Spartan existence, without cooking or hot water, but it allowed them to be close to the problems and to build trust with locals. "It gives us great agility," Hickey said at the time. They also worked with two thousand Iraqi soldiers to establish twenty-nine patrol bases throughout the city, providing a view of every major stretch of road. Hickey could then order attacks against insurgents from local patrol bases, rather than predictable raids from American bases. As the city began to stabilize, relations with the civilian population thawed. As the mayor told George Packer, "I began to work with the Americans here and saw a new picture." They ultimately recruited a provisional, 1,400 person police force, many from Tal Afar.

Effectively confronting insurgents hinged upon navigating power dynamics that were opaque from outside. Satellites, spy planes, informants, and the like proved to be a start, not the solution. Interestingly, beginning in 2007, the army even assigned teams of anthropologists to each of the twenty-six American combat brigades in Iraq and Afghanistan to better navigate the subtleties of tribal relations. The best insights about problems to be addressed often come from the worm's-eye view.

I was intrigued to learn that ideas at Pixar also typically originate from its employees' worldly observations and experiences. In Pixar's 2009 film, *Up,* the movie's centerpiece, an elderly widower named Carl Frederickson, encounters a dog named Dug wearing a special electronic collar that allows him to vocalize his thoughts. This comes as a shock to Carl who, before meeting Dug, hears a distant voice exclaiming, "I can smell you!" The production challenge was to make Dug and *Up*'s other talking dogs, including the Alpha, relatable. According to Bob Peterson, who cowrote and codirected *Up*, Dug's lines were an amalgamation of all the dogs he has owned. One repeating theme is that the dogs are always on lookout for squirrels, to the extent that if one dog sounds an alarm by saying, "Squirrel!" the dogs divert all of their attention in the direction of the reported squirrel. Peterson explained: "The distractibility of Dug (SQUIRREL!!) is based on a game I'd play with my dogs. On a hot day the dogs would be panting to cool themselves down. So, I'd jump in and pant along with them. Then I'd stop abruptly and pretend I'd seen something important. The dogs would do the same and go to attention along with me. Long pause. Then, everyone back to panting." Peterson also noticed that dogs have a unique capacity to shower love on people they were meeting for the first time. Hence, shortly after Dug meets Carl, the line: "My name is Dug. I have just met you, and I love you," as he jumps on Carl.

There is a heavy emphasis at Pixar on doing field research to find creative insights and inspiration. For example, the team that developed the movie *Cars* went on two trips with Michael Wallis, author of *Route 66: The Mother Road*. They went to racetracks, a Detroit auto show, and on long road trips across Route 66. "They saw the teepee-shaped motels and gas stations," Wallis told the *New York Times*. "They felt the wind through the winter wheat. They gulped it all in." At an old car-wrecker lot in Galena, Kansas, Joe Ranft, then head of Pixar's story group, stopped for a moment and studied it. And it was there that the idea for "Tow-Mater," the rusty tow truck and beloved *Cars* character, was born.

Meanwhile, the crew working on *Finding Nemo* took several scuba diving trips to Monterey and Hawaii. They studied underwater reefs, sea life, fish movements, and how light passed through water at different depths. Pixar also hired Adam Summers, a professor and fish specialist, to give twelve lectures on the subject. "They were infinitely curious about fish, and they were flat-out the best students I had ever had," Summers shared. "By the end of each lecture, they would be asking me questions that I didn't have answers for."

* * *

Research evidence suggests a strong link between inquisitiveness and creative productivity. In an extensive six-year study about the way creative executives in business think, for example, Professors Jeffrey Dyer of Brigham Young University and Hal Gregersen of INSEAD, surveyed over three thousand executives and interviewed five hundred people who had either started innovative companies or invented new products. They also examined the habits of twenty-five exemplary innovators in depth, including the likes of Steve Jobs, Amazon's Jeff Bezos, VMWare's Diane Greene, and A. G. Lafley of Procter & Gamble.

The authors found several "patterns of action" or "discovery skills" that distinguished the innovators from the noninnovators, which in addition to experimenting, as we've seen, included observing, questioning, and networking with people from diverse backgrounds, all of which, Dyer and Gregersen believed, can be developed. As Gregersen wrapped up their findings: "You might summarize all of the skills we've noted in one word: 'inquisitiveness.' "

Dyer and Gregersen found that, like Yunus the anthropologist, exemplar innovators closely observed details, particularly about other people's behaviors. "In observing others, they act like anthropologists and social scientists," Dyer and Gregersen wrote in their *Harvard Business Review* study summary (co-authored with Harvard Business School Professor Clayton Christensen). The authors frequently cite Steve Jobs, who is well known around Silicon Valley for constantly studying the world for ideas.

Leander Kahney, author of *Inside Steve's Brain*, captures Jobs' insatiable curiosity well. Jobs noticed the first graphical interface on a visit to Xerox's PARC research center in 1979, which would later inform the Macintosh's interface. Apple's former CEO, John Sculley, recalled Jobs returning from a trip to Sony in Japan with one of the first Walkmans: "Steve was fascinated by it, so the first thing he did was take it apart and look at every single part. How the fit and finish was done. How it was built."

"Creativity is just connecting things," Jobs told *Wired* magazine. "When you ask creative people how they did something, they feel a little guilty because they didn't really do it, they just saw something. It seemed obvious to them after a while. That's because they were able to connect experiences they've had and synthesize new things. And the reason they were able to do that was that they've had more experiences or they have thought more about their experiences than other people ... Unfortunately, that's too rare a commodity. A lot of people in our industry haven't had very diverse experiences. So they don't have enough dots to connect, and they end up with very linear solutions without a broad perspective on the problem."

Take one of Steve Jobs' oft-used examples of connecting experiences and ideas, cited by Dyer and Gregersen. It began when Jobs dropped out of Reed College during his first year, but stuck around campus and decided to take a class in calligraphy. "It was beautiful, historical, artistically subtle in a way that science can't capture, and I found it fascinating," Jobs recalled in a commencement speech at Stanford University. Jobs never expected the experience to have practical applications, but it did ten years later when Jobs and Steve Wozniak were developing Apple's first Macintosh computer. "It was the first computer with beautiful typography. If I had never dropped in on that single course in college, the Mac would never have had multiple typefaces or proportionally spaced fonts."

Some investors have achieved significant advantages by embracing the value of immersion. Most investors sit all day in offices in London, New York, or Boston. In contrast, James Chanos, who runs Kynikos Associates and famously predicted Enron's and Tyco's fall, regularly sends analysts to attend industry trade shows to speak with sales reps working on the front lines to get an up-to-date pulse on market activities.

Truth be told, most investors get their insight from traders or other investors. It's what Chanos calls the *smart-guy syndrome*: When hedge-fund analysts go to a dinner in New York or London and hear someone they think is smart talk about a company. "The next day, they all go take a two percent stake in the company," Chanos says. This is not original thinking. It's amazing how common the smart-guy syndrome is among investors and how rare it is to find original thinking investors. In my experience, the best investors, by contrast, are contrarian thinkers. They get out into the world to find unique insights.

Similarly, comedians rely on keen observations to come up with new material. Jerry Seinfeld's greatest asset as a comedian may well be his acute observation skills. For his 2001 stand-up tour, his finished jokes were about Starbucks, construction sites, nose hairs, and a popular advertising slogan for Just for Men hair coloring products: "Look so natural, no one can tell." Musician John Legend also makes use of a constant process of careful observation, drawing on what he calls his "database" of details noted from his travels and relationships, as well as movies, TV, books, from all aspects of his life. This correlation between being open to experience and creativity is, in fact, one of the most prominent findings that threads throughout the creativity research.

The exemplars Dyer and Gregerson highlighted were also

voracious questioners, regularly seeking to challenge the status quo by asking "what if?" "why?" and "why not?" The authors wrote that the innovators steer "entirely clear" of what's called the *status quo bias*. This research demonstrates that people do not like to change unless there is a compelling reason to do so, such as an attractive incentive. Related research shows that people exhibit strong "loss aversion," in that they are twice as likely to seek to avoid losses as they are to acquire gains. The researchers who discovered this phenomenon found that people wanted to be able to gain at least forty dollars on a coin toss before they risked losing twenty dollars, a roughly two to one (fear-of-loss to pleasure-of-gain) ratio. Dyer and Gregersen noted, for example, the idea for Dell Computer initially sprang from Michael Dell, founder and CEO, asking why a computer should cost five times as much as its parts. "I would take computers apart . . . and would observe that $600 worth of parts were sold for $3,000," Dell shared. In laboring over the question, Dell's personal-computing business model ideas emerged.

The power of asking probing questions like these emerges time and again in studies of successful innovators. Those who observe Jeff Bezos find his ability to ask "why not?" as much as "why?" to be one of his most advantageous qualities. "When something seems like an opportunity—it seems like you have the skills, and maybe some kind of advantage, and you think it's a big area—you will always get asked the question, 'Why? Why do that?' Bezos told *Harvard Business Review,* then elaborated, "But 'Why not?' is an equally valid question. And there may be good reasons why not—maybe you don't have the capital resources, or parts of your current business require so much focus at this key juncture that it would be irresponsible. In that case, if somebody asked, 'Why not?' you would say, 'Here's why not . . .' But that question doesn't get asked." That's why, borrowing a phrase from my friend Ryan Jacoby, an associate partner at IDEO: *Questions are the new answers.*

Dyer's and Gregerson's findings and observations frequently reminded me of the ways in which I observed entrepreneurs operating when I worked in venture capital. Although you've probably never heard of him, when it comes to creating opportunities in unknown territory, Chet Pipkin is something of a master. He began teaching himself how when he was sixteen years old, on what could be called the other side of the tracks from downtown Los Angeles. As the founder and CEO of Belkin, a company that produces a wide range of computer accessories, Pipkin is one of that rare breed who is able to both start a company without outside funding and guide it through numerous growth phases past $1.0 billion in annual sales. He started the company in his parents' garage, making cables, and today you probably own a Belkin component or accessory for your iPod, computer, or home.

At Summit Partners, the venture capital firm where I worked which had invested in Belkin, Pipkin was one entrepreneur who everyone, including the toughest-minded partners, respected. One summer, I worked with Chet and a supporting team to develop the initial stages of a new market opportunity. I was able to experience how he thinks and acts from the trenches (the initiative has since become a large part of Belkin's business).

Chet suggested that I spend only a week or so doing market research, so that I could come up to speed on the industry and competitive landscape. His main advice was that we should just get out, talk with potential customers, and look for problems and needs before coming up with any strategies. Not surprisingly, he learned this approach through experience. When Chet first developed a burning desire to start a business as a teenager, he did not know specifically what he would (or could) do. No, he did not have a big idea. He was sixteen years old and still in high school. So, he spent what free time he had looking for ideas along Hawthorne Avenue, a street in Los Angeles with miles of strip malls through middle- and lower-middle-class suburbia. With next to no skills and no resources, Chet considered starting a landscaping service, a Baskin-Robbins franchise, a Rent-a-Santa business, a limo service, and a funeral home. But the limited growth prospects bugged him until he zeroed in on the personal computer industry. This was the early 1980s, when the industry was still in its infancy and computers were just beginning to make it into offices. It was a free-for-all.

One of Chet's friends, with whom he reenacted Civil War battles, helped him get a job at Electrosonic, a manufacturer and wholesaler of electronic components. Chet's job was to box computer connectors. He remembers, "I didn't know anything about hardware, I didn't know anything about software, I didn't know anything about computers. I didn't know anything." Yet he wanted to know what the products did so he started reading product catalogs. He would then make recommendations about pairing different items for shipment. Managers responded. Chet began to come to a realization that grew quickly: "Anybody can do this. *You just need to ask the right questions.*" [emphasis added.]

During evenings or on weekends, he visited computer stores to window shop and ask questions. He'd go to places like Radio Shack, Computer Land, Business Land, Microage, Jade, or Computer Point. He tried to get to know the store staff. Some wouldn't have time for him, especially at the bigger chains, but he would befriend owners at smaller stores. Chet watched what people were buying, searching for problems he could help solve. He especially wanted to know what questions they asked. Soon he discovered a problem. "It hit me like a two-by-four across the head," he recalls.

People might come into the store wanting to automate accounting for their business. So they would buy their first personal computer, some accounting software, a monitor, a box of disks, and a printer. Then, the person would ask, "Well, how do we hook up the printer?" The store might have cables in the back or people would have to go to Radio Shack. "I knew a little bit about cables from Electrosonic. And when I say a little, it was really a little. But it was something," he says, "and people needed these cables."

He didn't think it would be too difficult to fill the gap. So, he taught himself how to make cables, then acquired the necessary connectors and materials to produce a batch of ten. He took the completed ones to Ralph at Computer Stock, who bought them. Chet wasn't sure if he made a profit since it was only later that he figured out how much the cables cost to build, but he had discovered an opportunity, and Belkin Corporation was soon born.

All of this helps explain why, increasingly, the observational methods of anthropology are infiltrating the corporate world. Take an experience of Procter & Gamble's in Latin America. A large part of P&G's audience in Mexico are low-income people, the middle 60 percent of wage earners, a different demographic from its core market in the United States. There was a disconnect. Not surprisingly, the company experienced a number of failures there throughout the 1980s. In one instance, they launched a new low-suds detergent line in Mexico, called Ariel Ultra, that they assumed would be a hit because it saved people money and valuable storage space, only to find that it flopped. Why? Because many of its Mexican customers did manual labor and were very sensitive to perspiration odors as they rode busses home from work. What gave them comfort that their clothes were getting clean was seeing their detergent foam, something Ariel Ultra lacked. No suds meant not clean. The disconnect was reminiscent of why military strategies fail when they're not targeting the right problems.

P&G responded brilliantly. Under CEO A. G. Lafley who, by all accounts, balanced an appreciation for anthropology and economics, the company launched a program to have its employees actually live with representative users, called "Living It." P&G ethnographers, and also senior managers, spend time in low-income homes around the world to better understand what matters in their lives, including their desires, aspirations, and needs. (P&Gers also spend time searching for similar insights in stores, like Chet Pipkin did, what they called "Working It.") These insights then fueled the P&G idea development process, including laundry detergent with more noticeable suds.

These findings raise an important question: Why are some people voracious questioners and others are not? Exploring the drivers of inquisitiveness, Gregersen and Dyer gathered interesting insights about our approach to education. "If you look at four-year-olds, they are constantly asking questions and wondering how things work," Gregersen observed generally. "But by the time they are six and a half years old they stop asking questions because they quickly learn that teachers value the right answers more than provocative questions." It's a haunting finding that raises serious concern about our education system. Specifically, what is the purpose of education? Is it to convey knowledge, as the current system is weighted, or it to inspire and nurture an ability to constantly learn?

Probing into this puzzle, Gregersen and Dyer were intrigued to learn that a number of the innovators in their study went to Montessori schools, where they learned to follow their curiosity. The Montessori learning method, founded by Maria Montessori, emphasizes self-directed student learning, particularly for young children. Well-known Montessori alums include Google's founders Sergei Brin and Larry Page, who credit their Montessori education as a major factor behind their success, Jeff Bezos, and computer game pioneer Will Wright, as well as Julia Child.

The innovators got encouragement to pursue their intrinsic interests from parents, teachers, neighbors, other family members, and the like. As Gregersen shared, "We were struck by the stories they told about being sustained by people who cared about experimentation and exploration." It's a powerful finding that emerges time and again. Instead of placing significant value on external measures of achievement, parents of those who become successful creatives tend to emphasize pursuing whatever interests they have. Pixar's Chief Creative Officer John Lasseter, for example, was interested in cartoons from a young age and was encouraged by his mother to pursue drawing them as a career, starting with art school. The singers and songwriters I interviewed, including John Legend and Kevin Brereton, were heavily influenced during childhood by their families' extensive music collections.

That's not to say that the parents of highly successful creative types don't have high expectations for their kids. They do. But, as with John Lasseter, John Legend, or Kevin Brereton, their parents tend to support their kids' natural pursuits, while also stressing work ethic and quality. These patterns, ironically enough, tie back to Carol Dweck's findings on fixed versus growth mind-sets; fostering a questioning mind is also fostering one that is predisposed to a growth perspective. The implications for parents and educators are significant and worthy of further research.

For those of us who are already grown up, acting like anthropologists is one of the most powerful ways to help us formulate the questions that will uncover invaluable insights and answers. And in so doing, it's important not only to dive deep into particular, selected environments, as Muhammad Yunus did, but also to go wide.

CHAPTER 7

Learning a Little
from a Lot

Frank Gehry's early designs were fairly conventional buildings, like shopping malls and suburban houses, a far cry from
the stainless steel metallic exterior at the Guggenheim Museum in Bilbao or Disney Hall in Los Angeles. He discovered
his unique style later in life, thanks in part to a handful of artists he got to know during the 1950s and 1960s. "The biggest
influence on the design of my houses was Robert Rauschenberg," Gehry says in *Sketches with Frank Gehry*. As a pioneer
of abstract art known as Neo-Dadaist, Rauschenberg would
use everyday objects that he'd find strewn on the streets of
New York City in his art, things like pieces of crumpled newspaper, metal fans, or trash. Gehry brought these ideas into
his own work starting with his own home in Santa Monica,
California, where he experimented with plywood, corrugated
sheet metal, and chain-link fencing, and literally built a new
exterior around the original house. It was the beginning of
what would become his distinctive style of architecture.

Gehry's experience with Rauschenberg illustrates the remaining pattern of action that Dyer and Gregersen found dis-

tinguished the innovators from the noninnovators that we haven't yet covered: innovators routinely networked with people who came from different backgrounds. It's a way to challenge one's assumptions and gain broader insight. For Dyer's and Gregersen's research pool of creative executives, the people who were sources of inspiration might include artists, academics, scientists, politicians, or adventurers.

Indeed, Dyer's and Gregersen's finding mirrors a preponderance of evidence that indicates that diversity, be it of perspectives, experiences, or backgrounds, fuels creativity. We see this pattern at the individual, organizational, and societal level. Professor Keith Sawyer of Washington University summarized the topic well in his book *Group Genius*. Meanwhile, Frans Johansson's book, *The Medici Effect*, builds on major pillars of psychology research to demonstrate how diverse teams are more likely to be innovative. University of California Berkeley Professor AnnaLee Saxnian and author Richard Florida have produced compelling analyses about how cities and regions with diverse workforces (from a functional standpoint) and frequent interpersonal interactions are more innovative. Here I want to focus on the very specific, yet oft-neglected, value of learning from people who have different perspectives. One person in particular came to my mind repeatedly.

Before passing away suddenly (and shockingly) June 13, 2008, Tim Russert was one of the most prominent American political journalists and commentators of his generation, including as the moderator of NBC's weekly *Meet the Press*. The son of a sanitation worker from Buffalo, Tim would always embrace his working-class roots and was described as "the anchor of everyman." My mother had been friends with Tim's wife, Maureen Orth, for years. Maureen, who would go on to become a prominent journalist for *Vanity Fair*, began her career as a reporter in the Bay Area, during which time Mom took photos for Maureen's stories.

In 1987, my family visited Tim and Maureen in New York City before we embarked on a car camping tour through New England. At the time, Tim was working as an executive at NBC News, four years before he would become a known TV personality as host of *Meet the Press*. Tim and Maureen took us to dinner at one of their favorite Italian restaurants and Tim treated my brother Christo (then eight) and me to root beers and asked us questions all night.

We would see Tim at most once per year after that, but every time we did, he was always interested in talking with us kids. Tim and Maureen would come to San Francisco for Christmas most years and would host a small gathering for their old friends from the area. There would be, say, twenty or thirty people there, including McKinsey consultants and the like, yet Tim would spend at least half the time talking with the kids. Christo and I could never quite believe this, especially as Tim became more and more well-known (and we became old enough to recognize it). But he always treated us with utmost respect, asked us tons of questions, and *really listened*. He was genuinely interested in our opinions and was also very open about what he thought about a topic or person, say a particular member of Congress.

In fact, Tim unleashed this voracious curiosity in conversations with nearly everyone he encountered. From senators and statesmen, to his father's friends at American Legion Post 721 in Buffalo, to kids who didn't know their asses from their elbows. Learning a little bit from a lot of people was one of the main ways Tim identified so many unique ideas and insights. He left no stone unturned and was extremely open to what could emerge from each interaction.

*   *   *

While Tim had demonstrated that you can "learn a little bit from a lot of people" for years, it was eBay's CEO, John Donahoe, who first introduced me to the expression. Donahoe mentioned it in the context of his development as a leader, an approach he had learned from his father. Donahoe's point was that people too often have a tendency to think that certain people, experts or mentors for example, have all the answers when in reality insight is far more dispersed. Donahoe says he practices this in every meeting. The cumulative insight Donahoe gathers compounds over time and, presuming John's judgment is as good as it seems, gives him a competitive advantage.

Most CEOs in Donahoe's generation, although certainly not all, would agree that the best decisions and ideas depend upon gathering and culling insights from a wide variety of people. This was not always the case. One of the most influential management fads during the 1980s was the idea of management by walking around. The term itself was based on the way David Packard managed at Hewlett-Packard. Packard got out of his office and walked around to talk with and listen to HP's employees. Bill Hewlett worked in a similar manner. He regularly ate lunch and talked at length with HP's engineers about what they were working on. Gathering insights from people doing the work seems like such an obvious (and fairly common) way to be a better-informed leader and person, but in the early 1980s, it wasn't a mainstream management practice. In their landmark book, *In Search of Excellence*, Tom Peters and Bob Waterman enthused about the idea. Numerous strands of leadership research and publications built on this tradition, including Jim Collins' book, *Good to Great*. Great leaders, Collins argued, need to be able to actually listen, which requires a degree of humility that Pixar's president Ed Catmull exemplifies. Naturally, leaders' assumptions are only as accurate and relevant as their experiences.

Stepping back for a moment, let's consider Tim Russert's desire to learn a little bit from a lot of people through two lenses. Along one dimension, Tim exhibited a great openness to ideas and insights from a wide variety of people. This behavior correlates with one of the most consistent findings from the psychology research over the past thirty years about creative thinkers and doers, what researchers call "openness to experience." Those who have studied the differences between creative and eminent scientists and their less creative and eminent peers have produced similar conclusions.

That creative people are more open to ideas and experiences seems like an obvious finding. However, it's critically important to emphasize the point since there are so many forces at work that create rigidities be it within our organizations, social networks, or broader society. This is the status quo bias in action. Ironically, despite being one of the most knowledgeable people in his field, Tim was constantly open to new information and ideas from an extremely diverse network of people. This is a critical capacity that anyone can develop. In order to get a better understanding of the value of doing so, let's turn to the research of Dr. Richard Wiseman, who runs a research unit at the University of Hertfordshire in the United Kingdom and spent ten years studying why some people seem to be lucky, while others seem to be unlucky.

To understand whether different behavioral patterns characterized lucky versus unlucky people, Wiseman performed a series of experiments on four hundred people, and summarized his findings in his book *The Luck Factor*. His study sample included people from all walks of life, ranging in age from eighteen to eighty-four, including secretaries, doctors, computer analysts, factory workers, and businesspeople.

Wiseman and company began by surveying people about whether they perceived themselves to be lucky or unlucky. They found that 50 percent of the respondents considered themselves to be lucky, 36 percent felt they were neither lucky nor unlucky, while fourteen percent said they were consistently unlucky. So, for example, a forty-two-year-old forensic scientist named Jessica exemplified someone in the "lucky" group. "I have my dream job, two wonderful children, and a great guy whom I love very much. It's amazing; when I look back on my life, I realize I have been lucky in just about every area," Jessica shared.

Meanwhile, a thirty-four-year-old care assistant named Carolyn epitomized someone in the "unlucky" group. As Wiseman wrote, "She is accident-prone. In one week, she twisted her ankle in a pothole, injured her back in another fall, and reversed her car into a tree during a driving lesson. She was also unlucky in love and felt she was always in the wrong place at the wrong time."

Over the next several years, Wiseman sought out differences between these self-described "lucky" and "unlucky" people. He performed in-depth interviews, asked people to complete diaries, and administered a battery of tests, experiments, and questionnaires. So, for instance, in one experiment, Wiseman gave both self-described lucky and unlucky people a newspaper and asked them to count the number of photographs it contained. He found that it took people in the unlucky group roughly two minutes to complete the task, whereas it took people in the lucky group just seconds. "Why?" Wiseman recounts, "Because the second page of the newspaper contained the message: Stop counting. There are forty-three photographs in this newspaper." The message took up a half a page and the typeface was more than two inches high, nearly impossible to miss. According to Wiseman, "It was staring everyone straight in the face, but the unlucky people tended to miss it and the lucky people tended to spot it." Even more, as Wiseman describes it, "For fun, I placed a second large message halfway through the newspaper: 'Stop counting. Tell the experimenter you have seen this and win £250.' Again, the unlucky people missed the opportunity because they were still too busy looking for photographs."

As the newspaper photo counting experiment illustrates, one obvious implication from Wiseman's research is that lucky people pay more attention to what's going on around them than unlucky people. It's more nuanced than that. Here's where being open to meeting, interacting with, and learning from different types of people comes in. Wiseman found that lucky people tend to be open to opportunities (or insights) that come along spontaneously, whereas unlucky people tend to be creatures of routine, fixated on certain specific outcomes.

In analyzing behavior patterns at social parties, for example, unlucky people tended to talk with the same types of people, people who are like themselves. It's a common phenomenon. On the other hand, lucky people tended to be curious and open to what can come along from chance interactions. For example, Wiseman found that the lucky people had three times greater open body language in social situations than unlucky people. Lucky people also smiled twice as much as unlucky people, thus drawing other people and chance encounters to them. They didn't cross their arms or legs and pointed their bodies to other people and increased the likelihood of chance encounters by introducing variety. Chance opportunities favored people who were open to them.

Wiseman believed another type of behavior played an even greater role in success. Wiseman found that lucky people build and maintain what he called a strong *network of luck*. He wrote:

> Lucky people are effective at building secure, and long-lasting, attachments with the people they meet. They are easy to know and most people like them. They tend to be trusting and form close relationships with others. As a result, they often keep in touch with a much larger number of friends and colleagues than unlucky people. And time and again, this network of friends helps promote opportunity in their lives.

This was Wiseman's core finding: You can create your own luck. "I discovered that being in the right place at the right time is actually all about being in the right state of mind," he argued. Lucky people increase their odds of chance encounters or experiences by interacting with a large number of people. Extraversion, Wiseman found, pays opportunity and insight rewards. And that makes perfect sense: Chance opportunities are a numbers game. The more people and perspectives in your sphere of reference, the more likely good insights and opportunities will combine, as they often did for Tim Russert.

How specifically did learning a little bit from a lot of people help Tim to be an original thinker? Consider this example. The last time I saw him was in October 2006. I was in Washington for a conference and Tim and Maureen took me and another family friend, Daniel Kilduff, to Tesoro for dinner, one of Tim's favorite Italian restaurants in Washington. By then, Tim was a household name, one of the most known and trusted political commentators in the United States. He was the author of two *New York Times* best-selling books and made regular appearances on NBC's *Today Show,* as well as programs on its cable affiliate CNBC. Perhaps most memorably, on election night 2000, with George W. Bush and Al Gore locked in the tightest presidential race in history, Tim held up a small dry-erase board, with red ink scribbles that read, "Florida. Florida. Florida." It would all come down to Florida, he predicted.

That night, Tim was extremely curious to hear some outside Washington views. Again, this was October 2006, more than two years before the next presidential election. Tim began by asking for our impressions about a wide range of potential presidential candidates from both parties.

The question was timely because Daniel had some perceptive insight about North Carolina senator John Edwards. At the time, Senators Hillary Clinton and John McCain were the most likely Democratic and Republican nominees respectively. Tim told us that many Washington observers believed that Edwards (a Democrat) and Massachusetts Governor Mitt Romney (a Republican) were the dark-horse candidates from each party. Edwards had recently visited Stanford University where Daniel was finishing a masters program, and Daniel told us that his Stanford classmates felt like Edwards was phony. They felt he was too worried about his hair and after meeting him up close, they even wondered whether he might be using fake tanning substances. "That's really interesting," Tim said. That night was nearly three years to the day before Edwards' dramatic fall, when he admitted publicly to lying about an affair for the first time. Edwards, in his own words, attributed his behavior to "a self-focus, an egotism, a narcissism that leads you to believe that you can do whatever you want." The Stanford students saw the signs long before the Beltway conventional wisdom did.

This back-and-forth continued for a while, covering candidate by candidate, during which time Tim also discussed his own insights and questions about each one. One question seemed foremost on his mind. Would Barack Obama, then a second-year U.S. senator, run for president? Obama was scheduled to appear on *Meet the Press* two weeks later and, on that Friday night, whether Obama was considering a presidential run was very much an open question.

On one hand, Obama appeared to be leaning against a run. Again, conventional Washington wisdom suggested that while Obama was certainly a rising political talent, running in 2008 would be too early. Having only served for two years in the senate, Obama lacked the experience that Hillary Clinton possessed, and Clinton was already the odds-on favorite for the Democratic nomination. Additionally, on Obama's last *Meet the Press* appearance in January, he flatly dismissed speculation that he would run for president in 2008.

Yet, even though he said he wouldn't run, Obama was clearly working hard to build his national profile. For several months, he had been crisscrossing the country to promote his second book, *The Audacity of Hope*, while helping dozens of congressional candidates to raise money. So, Tim asked: "What do you guys think?"

Before flying to Washington, by chance I was in an airport bookstore, flipping through some magazines. One of those was the September/October issue of *Men's Vogue*, which had a feature article about Obama. The article was mostly a puff piece, alongside photos by Annie Leibovitz, until a few paragraphs toward the end of the article. One in particular read:

Obama is well aware of the obstacles he would face, including his limited experience in foreign policy, and Hillary Clinton's embedded position as front-runner. It's also not lost on him that much of the next president's job will be "cleaning up the mess," which is as close as he comes to trashing the Bush administration. *"My attitude about something like the presidency is that you don't want to just be the president,"* *he continues.* *"You want to change the country. You want to make a unique contribution. You want to be a great president."* [Emphasis added.]

Hmmm . . . That quote sounded an awful lot like Obama might be seriously weighing a presidential run. Why else would he be thinking so much about the presidency as a second-year U.S. senator? So, when Tim asked us what we thought, I mentioned it. *"Men's Vogue?!"* he asked with a laugh, as if wondering how anyone would find useful political insight in a fashion magazine. Ha, ha, ha . . . I know, I know . . . After a pause, Tim raised his eyebrows, and said, "Interesting . . ." After a bit more back and forth, he offered, "I think he might run." But Obama would soon have a lot of explaining to do.

Two weeks later, on the October 22, 2006 episode of *Meet the Press*, he began the interview with Obama by asking a handful of questions about the Iraq War and other foreign policy issues, before transitioning to the elephant in the room. The transcript reads:

RUSSERT: You told *Vogue, Men's Vogue* magazine, that if you wanted to be president, you shouldn't just think about being president, that you should want to be a great president. So you've clearly given this some thought.

SEN. OBAMA: Yes.

After asking Obama several questions about his lack of experience, Russert pushed him for a more precise position about whether he was weighing a run for president. Moments later, despite his position in January, Obama would, for the first time, open the door to a possible presidential run.

SEN. OBAMA: Well, the—that was how I was thinking at that time. And, and, you know, I don't want to be coy about this, given the responses that I've been getting over the last several months, I have thought about the possibility. But I have not thought it—about it with the seriousness and depth that I think is required. My main focus right now is in the [sic] '06 and making sure that we retake the Congress. After, oh—after November 7, I'll sit down and, and consider, and if at some point, I change my mind, I will make a public announcement and everybody will be able to go at me.

RUSSERT: But it's fair to say you're thinking about running for president in 2008?

SEN. OBAMA: It's fair, yes.

Obama's acknowledgement that he was considering a run for president quickly became the day's breakthrough news and sent ripples through the political world. Tim was at the top of his craft for many reasons, but as in many professions, knowledge of diverse perspectives drives good journalism and original thinking. As any comedian or Frank Gehry will say, new insights, inspiration, and ideas are around us all the time, but they are not always obvious. Everyone from janitors to cab drivers to kids to experts has them. That's where being open and asking other people lots of questions comes in. Tim

Russert's interviews on *Meet the Press* were just the tip of a deep iceberg.

Wiseman took his research on luck one step further. After identifying a group of people who identified themselves as unlucky, he shared the main principles of lucky behavior, including specific techniques. As Wiseman described it, "For instance, they were taught how to be more open to opportunities around them, how to break routines, and how to deal with bad luck by imagining things being worse." Wiseman included exercises to increase chance opportunities, such as building and maintaining a network of luck, being open to new experiences, and developing a more relaxed attitude toward life, as well as ways to listen to hunches and to visualize lucky interactions. After carrying out specific exercises for a month, participants reported back to Wiseman. "The results were dramatic: eighty percent were happier and more satisfied with their lives—and luckier," Wiseman summed.

Just as Wiseman's research demonstrates that we can make our own luck, including by lowering our rigid expectations and being open to new ones, Tim Russert made his own luck. As a graduate of John Carroll University, that Tim didn't have a name-brand college background was a source of insecurity for him for many years. What compensated for this perceived lack of educational prestige were his instincts. When Senator Moynihan invited Tim to move from Buffalo to join his Washington staff, most of the senator's staff had Ivy League backgrounds. "I'm not sure I belong here," he told Moynihan. Moynihan didn't flinch, as Tim recalled in an interview, "And he said, 'You have to understand: What you know, they'll never know, and what they know, you can learn.' And he slapped me on the back, dusted me off, and sent me on my way."

Moynihan's comment points to an important issue regarding the value of getting out in the world and asking many questions; expert advice can be myopic and often wrong. That doesn't mean that experts should be avoided altogether. As we will see in the next chapter, there is a certain category of experts that can provide particularly valuable insights and feedback.

CHAPTER 8

Learning a Lot
from a Little

There's an important reason that stand-up comedians target small comedy club audiences with their little bets, and it's
backed up by decades of empirical research, including that
of MIT Professor Eric von Hippel. After all, places like the
Stress Factory or Stand Up New York are magnets for hardcore stand-up comedy aficionados. Recall that Chris Rock
watches the audience body language closely, especially the
die-hard regulars who typically sit in the center of the room,
and frequently makes notes about their reactions. Von Hippel
showed how these types of cutting-edge users of ideas provide
unique insight about what ideas will be valuable to a broader
audience. Seeking out a small group of these active users with
little bets is an astute way to tap into unique insights and
desires.

That new ideas travel along a curve of adoption from early
to late adopters is now widely accepted. Everett Rogers, the
late professor of communications and sociology at Ohio State
University, began researching how ideas spread in the 1950s.

Rogers began by studying how new ideas and techniques spread among Iowa farmers. By the 1960s, the area of research exploded, from studies about how new ideas originate and spread within and between social systems ranging from tribes in Africa to technology clusters in the United States. Extrapolating from these studies, Rogers coined the term *early adopters* to describe people who act as trendsetters for new ideas and solutions, people who have insights and preferences that foreshadow those of the masses. He developed his theory by watching how innovations spread along an S-curve of adoption, starting with innovators and early adopters, rising past a tipping point of popularity, before eventually reaching the broad masses, before gradually declining to reach a small number of laggards.

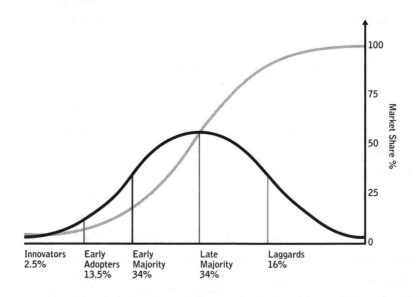

Today, Rogers's S-curve is ubiquitous and may be applied to the spread of anything, from technologies like iPads to the way new bands become popular to the rise of new words.

Rogers's research, and landmark book *Diffusion of Innovations*, informed *The Tipping Point* by Malcolm Gladwell, as well as an array of other books that examine how to better spread ideas, such as Geoffrey Moore's book *Crossing the Chasm*.

Countless other researchers built on Rogers's body of work, including Eric von Hippel, an economist and professor at the MIT Sloan School of Management, whose research added important insight. For decades, von Hippel has researched how insights from the most active early adopters (what Rogers called the *innovators*), such as the diehard stand-up audience members, help drive the early stage development of those ideas. Beginning in the 1970s, von Hippel examined where innovations come from (the original source of a later commercialized idea) across a range of industries, from scientific instruments to semiconductors to thermoplastics. In an extensive study on the sources of innovation for major scientific instruments, for instance, von Hippel found that one group, which he called *active users* or *lead users*, were responsible for developing over 75 percent of the innovations. A similar pattern ran across an array of other industries. These people not only serve as cutting-edge taste makers, they actively tinker to push and create new ideas on their own.

Since the needs of these active users precede and, according to the research, often anticipate, what the masses will like, they become incredibly valuable as idea development partners. The ideas they help generate can then be tested with broader audiences and commercialized. The same is true for good comedy. Weeknight comedy audiences have a thirst for fresh material. They've seen and heard it all, so they know what's good and what's not and are not afraid to voice their reactions.

Designers call these people *extreme users*, whose unique

needs can foreshadow the needs of other people. The reason why designers find extreme users so valuable is because the average person isn't actively thinking about solving problems like these. Their needs and desires are less pronounced. As mentioned previously, Steve Jobs will often say, "People don't know what they want until they've seen it."

Interestingly, many creative thinkers and doers use the von Hippel Strategy already, without knowing anything about von Hippel's findings. For example, singer and songwriter John Legend does so as he develops a new song. The first part of Legend's songwriting process is to develop a good back-beat working closely with music producers like Kanye West, will.i.am, or Raphael Saadiq. Once he's found a beat he likes, Legend will then develop melodies on top of it, often working at a piano, and finally write the lyrics. Kanye West, in particular, is a classic innovator and active user, constantly consuming and tinkering with music. Legend and others consider West to be a creative genius in many respects, with a well-tuned ear for what broader audiences will like. His early involvement in a song routinely drives later success. So, Legend will bounce ideas around with West at all stages of the process, especially at the beginning. It's strategic trial and error.

Kayne West is one of Legend's closest creative collaborators, but certainly not the only one. Once John's got a melody and lyrics he feels good about, he'll bounce a song off writers and producers, his road manager, and those at his record label, as well as his friends, family, and girlfriend. "You try to have a balance of experts and lay people," Legend sums.

Von Hippel's findings have withstood the test of time, both within academic circles, as well as, more compellingly, among practitioners. So, for instance, over the past several years, executives at Procter & Gamble, working closely with the Stanford d.school, modified their new idea development processes. P&Gers not only now do quick and dirty prototyping, they develop new product ideas with the most active users. Senior executive Chris Thoen, who leads P&G's Global Open Innovation, describes their approach simply: "Choose a few consumers that you really feel are the early adopters, test it with them, see what they like about it and what they don't like about it . . . And, if it appeals to them, use them to optimize it [the idea] further and then the laggards will follow." Thoen and other executives at Procter & Gamble have learned the value of developing their ideas with active users through experience and from the field of design thinking. Until recently, this was not common practice.

That's in part because it stands in contrast to traditional market research. Mainstream market research used to emphasize asking people what they wanted, but I have yet to encounter an executive who thinks traditional market research works for identifying new ideas. They agree with Steve Jobs. So, it's not surprising that market-research techniques are rapidly evolving, thanks in large part to the emerging influence of design thinking approaches from ethnography and anthropology. Thus, marketers increasingly recognize the value of seeking out active users and showing them works in progress to develop opportunities and ideas and to see how they react. Then, as ideas get closer to completion, from laundry detergent to a Pixar film to a Chris Rock stand-up act, tests are done with broader audiences.

Von Hippel's research extended from these fundamental starting points with deep dives into how certain companies, namely 3M, could work with active users to develop new product innovations more effectively. 3M's effort began in the mid 1990s when managers there wanted to figure out how to improve the front it end of their idea development process: understanding and learning from what they called "bleeding edge" user needs. Working closely with von Hippel, executives in 3M's Medical-Surgical Markets Division embarked on a set of experiments to compare an active user strategy with 3M's traditional in-house idea generation approach which, essentially, was to allow product developers to develop their own ideas. The problem with this approach was that product developers focused mostly on incrementally improving existing products, rather than coming up with new, potentially breakthrough, ideas.

The results were compelling. Ideas generated from lead users weren't glitzy. They included things like new remote electronic and test communication equipment for telephone repair workers, as well as a new approach to replace foam peanuts when packaging fragile shipping items. A follow-up study published in 2002 found that using von Hippel's active user strategy to identify and develop ideas generated an average of $146 million after five years, more than eight times higher than the average project developed using traditional, in-house 3M idea-generation methods. (The researchers analyzed fifty years of 3M product development results.) Gradually, more 3M divisions began to adopt the active user approach.

As a leading example of these trends, computer giant SAP recognizes the unique value that its most active users can bring. Approximately 50 percent of SAP's service updates, released as enhancements to the core ERP software it sells, originate from its active users. What SAP did is set up what they call an *ecosystem* that allows its software users to connect online. Someone who uses SAP software as part of their job in the chemicals industry can connect online with other users in similar jobs, consultants, and SAP staff. They can ask questions, respond to others, or suggest modifications to the core software system. Think of it as a blog of blogs. Millions of users participate and thousands of bloggers comment regularly on questions. They also flag problems they experience using SAP software and recommend solutions. Von Hippel's findings helped pave the way for a growing wave of open innovation in the corporate world.

Now, to adopt the von Hippel Strategy, one of the things that 3M had to figure out, and that Chris Rock must do when he sets out to develop his material, was how to find active users. Active users are rare, but von Hippel found that they sit at the top of pyramids of other people who are working to solve similar problems. For example, a 3M medical imaging team knew that there was growing interest in technology that could identify smaller early stage tumors. Thus, they networked (often by phone) to identify and recruit a handful of radiologists who were interested in that problem. And a few radiologists had, in fact, already developed small imaging innovations on their own. Naturally, the insights from these radiologists about the problems and potential solutions were extremely valuable to 3M.

Active users are all around us. Perhaps they're experts on a certain type of music, under-the-radar pharmaceutical products, a social problem, new advertising techniques, or mountain bike trends. Take the mountain bike. It wasn't invented by a person or company. In the mid-1970s, dozens of avid pro-am riders in northern California started making modifications to their bikes for off-road riding on local mountains. They replaced thin tires with thicker ones, reformulated the braking systems, and modified the bike frames (I would recommend the documentary *The Klunkerz*, if you're curious about the whole story.). The microtrend grew ever more popular amongst enthusiasts, such that, by the early 1980s, commercial producers had finally taken note. The market took off from there; by 2004, mountain bikes accounted for more than 65 percent of all bikes sold, or $58 billion in sales. Mountain biking was an enormous idea and market waiting to be discovered. Anyone learning from those early adopters would have seen it coming.

For another example of how lead users can be so helpful, consider how the idea for this book came together. When I was in the very early stages of developing my ideas, I sent rough Power Point sketches and a three-pager to two types of publishing people. One group was a handful of literary agents, people on the front lines of the publishing industry, who spend every day reading book proposals or trying to sell ideas to publishers. The other group was composed of fellow authors, people like Christopher Gergen, coauthor of *Life Entrepreneurs*, Ori Brafman, coauthor (with his brother Ram) of the *New York Times* best-selling books *Sway* and *Click*, or Chip Heath, coauthor (with his brother Dan) of the bestselling books *Made to Stick* and *Switch*. Doing so helped surface key problems and opportunities quickly.

I then identified potential agents the same way 3M identified active users: by looking at who represented authors of similar books, asking around, then sending the agents cold email introductions. I will never forget the first conversation I had with one of these agents. Though painful, it illustrates the value of the von Hippel Strategy. After sending a rough three-pager, the agent and I spoke for thirty minutes. It was a *long* thirty minutes. Looking back over my notes, after exchanging some brief pleasantries, here were her comments in chronological order, with my reactions and responses in parentheses:

- "I'm very interested in the subject of 'right-brained' thinking." (Great! Why is that? Oh, design thinking is gaining momentum right now and readers are trying to figure out how it works. Right.)
- "Chart that you show is *not* understandable." (Included a primitive circular chart to show how ideas evolve through iteration. Okay, it's a bit complicated.)
- "Interested in subtitle, *Little Bets*" (Ahhh! Say more. The title of the draft was *Experimental Innovation: Turning Little Bets into Breakthroughs.*)
- "I don't know. It's a catchy term that sounds achievable to readers and seems to be an important part of what you're talking about." (Interesting. I agree. Let me sleep on it.)
- "Don't understand chart." (Okay, I hear you. It's too complicated. I will can it.)
- "Simpler language," no jargon. (I'm there.)
- "The [Stanford] d.school is hip and cool." (Cool.) "Cool." (Cool.)
- Click. (Wow. It felt as though someone had punched me in the stomach, but at least I had learned a lot.)

Over a hamburger a few days later, Ori Brafman looked at the same three-pager for about three minutes then said, "I love it! You should call this *The Little Bets Book.*" It was as if he had solved the riddle and could now eat his lunch. Then, after taking a bite, he stared into the distance with a pensive expression, then turned back and said, "I am not using little bets right now, but I should be. It's a different way of thinking." After moving *Little Bets* from the subtitle to the title and focusing the central idea, the entire audience response suddenly changed. Not only did every agent want to work on the project, nearly everyone I talked with, from CEOs to friends from school to my uncle (who is a truck driver), liked the idea and found the thinking useful. Despite the fact that I had never developed a book proposal, let alone a new book idea from scratch, the von Hippel Strategy helped to both efficiently identify the core problems and develop the central idea.

Just as Chris Rock develops his new acts with small audiences of avid comedy fans or 3M develops new products with active users, we can all seek out the active users in our work and social sphere, and even use methods to reach out wider to find them, and begin regularly tapping into their highly valuable insights, desires, and opinions.

CHAPTER 9

Small Wins

As we begin to make use of these methods to develop new ideas, strategies, and projects, they combine to facilitate what organizational psychologist Karl Weick refers to as *small wins*. Weick defines a small win as "a concrete, complete, implemented outcome of moderate importance." They are small successes that emerge out of our ongoing development process, and it's important to be watching closely for them. Sometimes, a Chris Rock joke will provoke a torrent of laughter, but more often, a positive reaction will come in the form of a muted chorus of chuckles. That's a small win because Rock knows that he's found a theme that has the makings of a good joke, which he can then build upon. Small wins are like footholds or building blocks amid the inevitable uncertainty of moving forward, or as the case may be, laterally. They serve as what Saras Sarasvathy calls *landmarks*, and they can either confirm that we're heading in the right direction or they can act as pivot points, telling us how to change course.

In the acclaimed paper in which Weick described small wins, published in the January 1984 issue of *American Psychologist*, he used the example of how helpful it is for alcoholics to focus on remaining sober one day at a time, or even one hour at a time. Stringing together successive days of sobriety helps them to see the rewards of abstinence and makes it more achievable in their minds. Elaborating on the benefits of small wins, Weick writes, "Once a small win has been accomplished, forces are set in motion that favor another small win."

One of the best examples of how a series of small wins shaped a company's evolution is Pixar's emergence as an animated film company. Recall that Pixar originated as a computer hardware company, trying to create a market for its Image Computer. Ed Catmull was intent on making feature films, but that goal was clearly a long way off, if achievable at all. When he started on his quest, the technology to produce digitally animated films, especially a feature-length film, was believed to be years, if not decades, away. Naturally, most people thought he was nuts.

For years after Steve Jobs bought Pixar, the company lost money on its hardware, and by 1988, despite massive sales efforts, Catmull's team had sold only 120 Pixar Image Computers. This agonized Jobs, but he showed remarkable flexibility in pivoting from one strategy to the next in search of profits and breakthroughs: from high-end computer graphics hardware to software to digitally animated TV commercials. There was no road map. Everything they were doing was new, and tensions ran extremely high. Jobs was supporting Pixar's losses with a line of credit and a personal guarantee, and given that animation wasn't producing any sales, the division was especially vulnerable to Jobs pulling out the rug. As David Price describes in *The Pixar Touch*, "On repeated occasions in the late 1980s, Catmull barely dissuaded Jobs from shutting down the animation division."

However, amid all of the efforts Pixar was making, animation was the one team that began to show signs of promise.

What Ed Catmull and John Lasseter did, which enabled them to impress Steve Jobs enough to continue to support their efforts, was to demonstrate the value of computer-generated animation films in a series of small wins. Although Jobs knew that Catmull and John Lasseter ultimately aspired to produce a feature-length film, they didn't ask his approval of that mission. Instead, they proposed a series of short films, and, as Catmull had done with George Lucas before, they justified making them by arguing that they would help to sell Pixar's other products. Catmull's initial reasoning for *Luxo Jr.,* the first short film made after Steve Jobs bought Pixar in 1986, was that it would help promote Pixar's hardware products at SIGGRAPH, a large annual computer graphics conference. Catmull also justified the project as a test of the animation production software Pixar had under development called RenderMan.

Running just over a minute and a half, *Luxo Jr.* was considered a real breakthrough, especially for its emotional realism. Lasseter used the Luxo lamp sitting on his desk as inspiration for the story involving a large lamp (adult) and a small lamp (child) interacting as the small lamp plays with a ball. The two lamp heads swivel, as if talking to one another, accompanied by audible purrs and squeaks. Then the small lamp jumps on a ball and pops it, before hanging its lampshade (head), and squeaking sadly, as if disappointing a parent. When the lights went up, *Luxo Jr.* received a standing ovation from an audience of roughly six thousand people at SIGGRAPH, an important boost for Pixar's reputation and brand. As Price described the short film's success, "It was perhaps the first computer-animated film that enabled viewers to forget they were watching computer animation." (The Luxo lamp would, in fact, later become Pixar's logo, and appear before every Pixar film.) It was a small win for Pixar's business (and relative to the ambition to produce a feature film), but it felt big for Lasseter and Catmull, an indicator that Pixar was treading into very interesting territory.

By the next year, Pixar's hardware business was still struggling, yet RenderMan had become a promising new product development, allowing animators to generate and manipulate 3D digital images and graphics, although it was not yet commercialized. *Luxo Jr.*'s success compelled Jobs to allow Lasseter and several assistants to make another short film. This time, the rationale for the project was twofold: to demonstrate the Pixar Image Computer, as well as to show how RenderMan could generate highly complex digital images, helping to generate credibility and demand for the software.

Red's Dream ran four minutes. In order to premiere the film at SIGGRAPH, Lasseter and his team worked around the clock to finish it, sleeping under their desks for days on end. It was about a depressed unicycle in a bike shop, sporting a half-off sale tag. The unicycle dreamed of being in a circus act (to great applause and drum rolls!). The unicycle woke up back in the bike shop, only to realize that it was just a dream. Sadly bowing its head (the bike seat), the unicycle rolled slowly back to its corner of the store, with somber blues music playing in the background. Lasseter resisted a happy ending. Emotion seeped through. The crowd at SIGGRAPH loved it, and, once again, Pixar received rave reviews.

However, the continued poor performance of Pixar's core hardware business again threatened the future of the animation division. Animation wasn't generating any revenues, yet was still costing Jobs money. Soon after the release of *Red's*

Dream, Jobs once again considered shutting the division down. By 1988, he had invested tens of millions of dollars in Pixar, and when Catmull came to him proposing to make a new short film, to be titled *Tin Toy*, Jobs this time said that he wanted to see more about the film. David Price described the scene in *The Pixar Touch*:

> A skeptical Jobs came to Lasseter's office to hear the story. (Lasseter had gotten out of the hallway.) With Catmull and the animation group in attendance, the storyboards pinned on his wall, Lasseter went through the drawings and acted out the shots—much as story men had done on the Disney lot for decades. The stakes here, however, were higher. We knew that he wasn't just pitching for the film, he was pitching for survival of the group, said Ralph Guggenheim, who was managing the animation unit.

John Lasseter acted out the storyboards for the short film entitled *Tin Toy* for Steve Jobs and Ed Catmull, using a pointer to move from one to the next. Oh, to have been a fly on that wall! Jobs, of course, eventually allowed the short to go forward, a decision that would prove to be extremely wise. The nearly five-minute short film was about a baby playing with his toys, told from the perspective of a tin toy, appropriately named Tinny. Tinny is fascinated by the baby at first, then gets increasingly scared and frantic when the baby chases it and throws it around the room.

This short would score a much bigger win. It won the Academy Award in 1988 for Best Animated Short Film. The Oscar win not only invigorated Jobs' interest in Pixar's animation group, after which he quickly approved the production of another short, it also established Pixar's credibility within the film industry, including at Disney, where executives tried repeatedly (and unsuccessfully) to recruit Lasseter.

Over the next few years, Jobs gradually began to pivot Pixar toward digital animation. It turned out that the Pixar Image Computer would never expand beyond early adopters. The business was sold to Viacom in 1990 for $2 million. In March 1991, after the company lost $8.3 million in 1990, Jobs attempted to continue funding the company, but only after laying off thirty of its seventy-two employees and shutting down most operations beyond digitally animated TV commercials and RenderMan software development. Many Silicon Valley observers wrote Pixar off. Lasseter and the animation team, meanwhile, started generating revenue from TV commercials totaling $1.3 million in 1990 and $2.0 million in subsequent years. Ironically, animation became the only profitable part of the business and helped fund the RenderMan development.

By the early 1990s, Pixar's accumulated experience with short films and technology had attracted Disney's interest in partnering on a feature-length computer animated film. Lasseter used the short film *Tin Toy* as the basis for *Toy Story*, the first feature film that Disney would coproduce with Pixar and distribute in an agreement announced in May 1991. Ed Catmull's audacious dream would soon be realized.

Starbucks evolved in a similar manner. Remember that when Howard Schultz founded what would become Starbucks, the baristas wore bow ties, nonstop opera music played, and the store had no chairs. "We made a lot of mistakes," Schultz regularly acknowledges. Schultz and his team learned from them as they did from countless other experiments. Drawing upon his observations of Italian coffee houses, Schultz's grand vision was to create a different kind of coffee experience that he called the "Starbucks experience": where people could experience great coffee in a communal place. As for the specifics, the Starbucks store and experience of today looks almost nothing like Schultz's original concept.

The Starbucks we know emerged by carefully adapting to customer feedback through a series of small wins. In fact, Schultz described Starbucks's mentality as: "the value of dogmatism and flexibility." As long as ideas were in accordance with company principles, Schultz believed they should just say yes to customer requests. So, for example, Schultz was initially determined to avoid using nonfat milk since he didn't think it tasted as good as regular milk and because it was at odds with the Italian coffee experience. When customers kept requesting nonfat drinks, Schultz relented. The success of those drinks became an important small win and soon much more: nonfat milk would grow to account for almost half of Starbucks's lattes and cappuccinos. "In hindsight, the decision looks like a no-brainer," Schultz wrote in *Pour Your Heart Into It,* but that direction wasn't obvious; it was the fast pace of sales that proved the point.

Not even Schultz could have predicted that Starbucks's countless different types of lattes would eventually satisfy millions of previously unknown desires. By the 1980s, per capita coffee consumption had been declining for twenty years. Schultz and his colleagues persevered through the criticisms of countless naysayers, including most investors who dismissed the company's ideas. Small win by small win, they learned that people wanted affordable luxuries, in the form of two-dollar cappuccinos, and had a wide range of exotic tastes, such as for espresso macchiatos.

Some of the benefits of small wins are easy to appreciate. For one, as Weick described, they help to build momentum and can be the crucial boost to beat back the inevitable frustration of any creative endeavor. If Pixar's shorts hadn't produced some visible results, such as the SIGGRAPH response, Steve Jobs would have surely shut down the animation division. Small wins can also quiet the naysayers. Even though the early short films did not produce revenues, Jobs was open to seeing how the next one would unfold. Or take the case of agile software development. Recall that, in agile development, software emerges through an ongoing discovery process. Key to this is that developers seek out small wins to validate their direction. Once version 1.0 of a feature is released, developers look for evidence that customers either like the specific feature or to clarify the problems to be solved. Sometimes they must shift their focus completely. When the developers get positive feedback from users, customers are satisfied and more receptive to the next idea, and software developers are also more motivated because they've accomplished something they've seen get a good response. In addition, other stakeholders, such as managers or investors, gain confidence that the agile process is working effectively. According to Weick, "a series of wins at small but significant tasks . . . reveals a pattern that may attract allies, deter opponents, and lower resistance."

Another benefit of small wins is less immediately obvious: They enable the development of the means to attain goals. Recall from Saras Saravathy's research how important the development of means is to seasoned entrepreneurs. Entrepreneurs use their available means, such as their expertise, networks, or financial resources, to develop their ideas and access additional resources and means. One way that Ed Catmull (and later Steve Jobs) developed Pixar's means was by steadily bringing in new talent with complementary skills.

Catmull was a great technologist, but to accomplish his dream, he needed to attract people like Lasseter, with his expertise in animation and storytelling, and Alvy Ray Smith, with computer graphics expertise. The small wins that Catmull, Lasseter, Smith and the team made enabled them to bring in the steady stream of additional talent that allowed them to develop ever-improving technology, such as Render-Man animation software, and to build their reputation, becoming a distinctive digital animation brand.

They also continuously developed the ability to tell a good story. Each short became more emotionally nuanced and graphically realistic. The progressively developed technology and storytelling means were what convinced Disney to partner with Pixar for a full-length film, which provided the additional financial, production, and distribution means that Pixar needed in order to at last bet big and fulfill Catmull's bold vision.

We also clearly see how small wins enable the building up of means in the case of counterinsurgency strategy. For example, General McMaster might focus on retaking control of several city blocks from insurgents, then focus on holding civilian control of those blocks, not just on routing out insurgents from them—what army strategists describe as *consolidating gains*. The benefits of doing so are not only to maintain these positions and prevent safe harbors for insurgents, but in building larger support for the army's operations. As they make a neighborhood safer, they begin to accumulate allies in the community, facilitate an uptick in commerce, and recruit local advisors. This will bring them additional intelligence about insurgent activities. It also builds momentum for the participation of the civilian population in the larger operations, such as establishing a police force and municipal government infrastructure.

As Weick explains about this benefit of small wins, "New

allies bring new solutions with them and old opponents change their habits. Additional resources also flow toward winners, which means that slightly larger wins can be attempted."

One element of small wins that is particularly tricky to absorb is that very often they will not emerge in a linear fashion, so they cannot reliably be predicted or planned for and may not build on one another, one step after another. In some instances, one small win may clearly lead directly to another. This was the case for Ed Catmull and his team at Pixar. As Weick describes the unpredictable nature of small wins:

> It is important to realize that the next solvable problem seldom coincides with the next "logical" step as judged by a detached observer. Small wins do not combine in a neat, serial, linear form with each step being a demonstrable step closer to some predetermined goal. More common is the circumstance where small wins are scattered and cohere only in the sense that they move in the same general direction . . . A series of small wins can be gathered into a retrospective summary that imputes a consistent line of development, but this post-hoc construction should not be mistaken for orderly implementation.

Think of General McMaster's counterinsurgency approach. In gaining control of Tal Afar, the Army accomplished a diverse set of small wins not through a preordained step-by-step process, but as the troops simultaneously probed and observed the situation on many fronts. For example, they initiated the process of developing better relations with tribal leaders while also setting up their patrol bases and going on reconnaissance missions. Troops achieved small wins in all of these fronts gradually, over time, from gaining more and more trust among the tribal leaders and knowledge of the power structure, discovering the key choke points for the smuggling of supplies for the insurgents into the city, and identifying and containing more and more safe houses. For a time, the progress was not at all obvious, or that those successes would eventually add up to an accomplished mission. McMaster understood that they were conducting a discovery process and that each small win was significant.

One last, yet important, point about small wins is that often, rather than validating a direction we've been pursuing, they will provide a signal to proceed in a different way. In this way, small wins enable a flexibility about how to attain ultimate goals. It is much easier to decide to make a change of approach when we are doing so not because things aren't working but because something has started to work. This role as the facilitator of a change of course is obvious in the evolution of Starbucks, as small wins helped Schultz understand that he should pivot away from his original idea to model on Italian coffee houses and instead create a distinctive new American type of coffee house experience. If we think of the Pixar story from the perspective of Steve Jobs, who was looking for success not from the animated film team but from the divisions developing the company's hardware and software, then the small wins of Lasseter's team were key facilitators for the company's major pivot away from those businesses into becoming a film studio.

Given the dynamic quality of any discovery process, small wins provide a technique to validate and adapt ideas, to provide clarity amid uncertainty. In some cases, success comes through an accumulation of a series of small wins, such as Chris Rock's development of a new show. In other instances, small wins highlight places to change and pivot, as agile software releases routinely do. The key is to appreciate that we can't plot a series of small wins in advance, we must use experiments in order for them to emerge.

This brings us back to the fundamental advantages of the little bets approach; it allows us to discover new ideas, strategies, or plans through an emergent process, rather than trying to fully formulate them before we begin, and it facilitates adapting our approach as we go rather than continuing on a course that may lead to failure. Perhaps the crucial insight will come from a prototype, or maybe it's an observation through immersion or a small win that illuminates a subtle clue. It's not a linear process from step A to step B to step C. As Richard Wiseman's research demonstrates, chance favors the open mind, receptivity to what cannot be predicted or imagined based on existing knowledge. With the barriers lowered, the creative mind thrives on continuous experimentation and discovery.

CHAPTER 10

Conclusion

We're about back to where we began. We're taught to be linear thinkers—to follow pre-established procedures and plans—in a nonlinear world. If only the world were predictable. Middle East warfare is a metaphor for the extremely uncertain and unpredictable world in which we live. Jobs, careers, and valued skills mutate at unprecedented rates, driven by tectonic global shifts. Even mavens in Silicon Valley have trouble keeping up with the pace of technological change. Meanwhile, markets exhibit historic levels of volatility, which routinely drives investors crazy or away from investing altogether. Just as former Chairman of Federal Reserve Board Alan Greenspan acknowledged "a flaw" in his understanding of markets during the 2008 economic crisis, we cannot rely on past assumptions to predict the future. In this era, being able to create, navigate amid uncertainty, and adapt will increasingly be vital advantages.

There is another way. As we have seen, General McMaster, Chris Rock, Frank Gehry, agile software developers, Pixar animators, and seasoned entrepreneurs like Amazon's Jeff Bezos, Muhammad Yunus, and Belkin's Chet Pipkin all *do things to discover what to do.* At the core of this experimental approach, they use little bets to discover, test, and develop ideas that are achievable and affordable. Little bets are their vehicle for discovery, whereby action produces insights that can be analyzed, as Frank Gehry might when he builds a new prototype model, in order to identify, frame, and reframe problems and ideas, so that he can then adapt and act using little bets again.

To see all these principles in action, for instance, remember Chris Rock's approach. He watches the audience intently, noticing heads nodding, shifting body language, or attentive pauses, all clues about where good ideas might reside. He'll also improvise extensively to find new material. Most of the ideas fall flat. He may think he has come up with the best idea ever, but if it keeps missing with his audience, that becomes his reality. There will be five to ten lines during the night that work very well, which Rock can then build his act around. He can't know in advance which joke elements and combinations will work. He must try thousands of preliminary ideas out of which only a handful will make the final cut. By the time he reaches a big show, his jokes, opening, transitions, and closing have all been tested and retested rigorously. And the cycle repeats, day in, day out. Rock understands that ingenious ideas rarely spring into people's minds fully formed; they emerge through a rigorous experimental discovery approach.

It's important to recognize that Rock is not following a set of procedures. That would squelch his creativity. It's not as though Rock thinks to himself: "Okay, now I'm going to move from observing audience reactions to improvising new possibilities." Experimentation, careful observation, problem finding, and playful improvisation have all become part of his approach. He does these things simultaneously, in no particular order, not as a step one, step two, step three process. Because Rock's not self-conscious about a linear process, his mind is free to explore possibilities and to make novel connections. The more he practices using the approach, the more natural, intuitive, and expert he becomes.

Similarly, General McMaster lists such core counterinsurgency methods as: understand, act, assess and adapt, consolidate gains, and transition missions to civilian control. In the heat of the battle, he makes use of all of these elements concurrently. During training, McMaster can prepare his troops to understand in local cultures, for example, by learning how to go house to house for tea. Once on the ground, they must be able to continually evaluate and adapt, constantly framing and reframing problems as they come to better understand local power structures, customs, and insurgent capabilities. As new problems and experiments emerge, their plans evolve. It is not a linear process; it's a constant learning process. As General David Petraeus says about counterinsurgency operations, "The side that learns and adapts the fastest often prevails."

With that lack of predictability comes uncertainty and the unknown, which makes doing anything creative or original hard. *Dark valleys* are times when we are moving forward, at least we think we are, but there's no light to illuminate the destination. "I think it's necessary," Pixar director Pete Docter says about the inevitable self-doubt that accompanies any creative process. "On *Monsters Inc.*, I really wore that. I would come home at the end of a difficult day in story and I would think, 'I'm a fraud. I'm a failure. I don't know what I'm doing.' And now I realize, *well, that's the way it is!*"

Consider the experiences of Richard Tait, founder of the

board game company Cranium. Tait can relate to dark valleys viscerally. The memories bring grimaces even years later. His darkest days would arrive when Tait was in his thirties, but during his twenties, Microsoft was his home. "I don't even remember my twenties," he says. "I was probably working fourteen to sixteen hours a day. And I loved it. I was changing the world." He would respond to any challenge and became an in-house entrepreneur, with a contagious enthusiasm to ignite others to create new Internet businesses. Steve Ballmer, who would become Microsoft's CEO, noticed Richard, as did many other Microsoft executives. Richard became a superstar and was selected Microsoft's Employee of the Year in 1994.

However, the pace of technology change caused Richard to start to feel old almost overnight, certainly by 1996. "I went very quickly from being celebrated as employee of the year to being called old school." Microsoft's culture can be like that. It's extremely competitive when there's a target, like Apple or Google, but absent that, people can languish. That's how Richard felt. "The culture started to change. I wasn't the one in the meetings anymore." He wasn't working on the cool initiatives. He wasn't celebrated. "All of a sudden, I was old school," he recalls.

Tait opted to take some time off. "I was so lost." For three months, he goofed off. He rode motorcycles. He kicked a ball around, literally. He desperately wanted to feel productive again, to feel useful. Perhaps he could come up with a business idea of his own. But he had lost his muse. "I had no purpose, and without purpose I flail." The confusion weighed heavily upon him. "I need to feel like I'm making things." Yet he could not come up with any ideas.

Reluctantly, he went back to Microsoft, where he would stay for another two years. "They were really hard years."

After all, Tait had plenty of other things on his mind, besides wanting to create something new. He and his wife were in their early thirties and she was ready to have kids. "I couldn't really see how I was going to fit all that in." Being at Microsoft was slowly killing his soul. He had to leave. They had gotten the best from him.

For Tait, the darkest period had just begun. For the next six months, he worked to develop a business idea in the basement of his house. He wore his pajamas all day. "The only reason I was getting dressed was because my wife was coming home from work." He could no longer rely upon the Microsoft corporate armor for his identity. This was an extremely difficult transition. "I was hiding because people would ask me what are you working on because I was an ideas guy and I had nothing," he recalls. "When it's just Richard, it's so humbling and feels so vulnerable and naked." Richard felt depressed. The anxiety only made everything harder. He eventually got very sick, so sick he thought he had a tumor. It turned out to be a bad viral attack. "I was really disabled. I was shaking."

Fortunately, as Richard wandered, he was not alone. His wife, Karen, encouraged him to take his time. It was going to be okay. "I always say behind every great entrepreneur is a spouse rolling her eyes." Then there was his friend Bruno, a colleague from Microsoft. "He always said to me, 'You'll have another idea,' and just having somebody say that was enough." They started an investment company together that went nowhere but it gave Richard something to do. They had fun. Being with Bruno gave him confidence. "He's been my gladiator three times in my life." It was a sliver of light.

When the idea for Cranium finally struck, it came unexpectedly. Richard and Karen were visiting friends for a long holiday weekend. That Sunday was rainy, so the couples decided to play the board game Pictionary. Richard and Karen are so good at Pictionary that Karen hardly needs to draw a line before Richard could know it was an airplane. They won soundly. The other couple immediately wanted revenge and challenged Richard and Karen to a game of Scrabble. "My wife is very good, but I suck at Scrabble and Dan and Maggie keep their scores on the fridge. They humbled us."

Frustrated on the way home, humiliated even, Richard wondered why there wasn't a game where everyone could win. On the plane home, he sketched out the idea for a game with something for everyone: something for people who liked trivia, something for people who enjoy performing, something for people who love work. This became the core idea for the board game company, Cranium. After countless additional dark valleys and millions of games sold, Cranium's hallmark is still "Everyone Shines," where everyone can win.

For Richard Tait, his openness to ideas, growth-mindset perspective and determination, and willingness to continue to do things and work at it ultimately prevailed. For someone with a growth mind-set, a silver lining in Tait's character, a dark valley is a stepping stone to small wins. This is the little bets approach in action.

As we've seen, experimental innovators use strikingly similar methods inside their work processes. So, for example, they use lots of experiments and inexpensive prototypes to develop their ideas. Just as Frank Gehry uses crumpled sheets of paper to prototype rough building designs model after model after model, Chris Rock scribbles joke ideas on a notepad then reels off ideas in small clubs, not afraid to bomb with regularity. That's how he learns. Inside Pixar, the story is the same: they must use thousands of storyboards in order to develop a new film storyline and script. It's how they go from suck to nonsuck. Pixar directors understand what seasoned entrepreneurs like Jeff Bezos and agile software developers do: The faster they fail, the faster they will discover promising opportunities.

Along these lines, experimental innovators identify problems before solving them. So, unlike the top-down nature of cold warfare, General McMaster frames and reframes the key problems from the bottom up before taking bold action. Frank Gehry can easily relate: he must frame and reframe countless problems and ideas in order to design a building like Disney Hall from the inside out. Pixar animators do the same thing, using storyboards and work-in-progress reels to identify and fix problems like they did with the script for *Finding Nemo*. Identifying problems before solving them is also how seasoned entrepreneurs develop their ideas, just as Bill Hewlett encouraged in the early days at Hewlett-Packard.

To gather fresh insights and ideas, experimental innovators embrace a relentless curiosity. They get out and immerse into the world like Muhammad Yunus did when he subsumed himself in India's poverty to understand it from the worm's-eye view. It was here in the marrow of poverty where Yunus discovered the insights, ideas, and passion to fuel his little bets. The army uses virtually the same approach, acting like anthropologists as McMaster's troops did when they lived inside the city of Tal Afar, Iraq. Pixar researches its movies in a similar manner, such as a scuba-diving trip in advance of making *Finding Nemo* to get a sense for tropical fish, their movements, and their natural surroundings.

We could go on comparing the parallels, but the essential point is that it's not as though someone handed Chris Rock, Pixar's team, Chet Pipkin, General McMaster, or Frank Gehry a map and set of steps to follow; they learned their approach through their experiences. Creativity becomes a way of life. This then is the opportunity and invitation: little bets provide a powerful vehicle to approach life and work in a new way.

After all, as children we exhibit a natural desire to tinker, explore, and discover. Just examine research on child development. Starting soon after birth, experimenting and making mistakes are primary ways children learn and discover how things work. That tendency doesn't vanish when we become adults. As many researchers and observers have described, that innate curiosity which is the basis for so much creativity routinely gets squelched. Perfection is rewarded, while making mistakes is often penalized. The term "failure" has taken on a deeply personal meaning, something to be avoided at nearly all costs.

When it comes to our educational systems, perhaps the most important question that we can ask is this: What is the purpose of education? Is it to impart knowledge and facts or is it to nurture curiosity, effortful problem solving, and the capacity for lifelong learning?

Educational historians have repeatedly shown that today's schools were designed during the first half of the twentieth century to meet the demands of the industrial era, not an innovative knowledge economy. "Very few schools teach students how to create knowledge," says Professor Keith Sawyer of Washington University, a leading education and innovation researcher. "Instead, students are taught that knowledge is static and complete, and they become experts at consuming knowledge rather than producing knowledge." This is unacceptable.

Change happens in small, achievable ways. On a visit to

an experimental lab that teaches kids about design methods, I was struck by a simple example of this when a brown-eyed second grader asked her teacher, "Are there pencils in this classroom?" Now, I don't know about you, but my second grade teacher would have just pointed to the pencils. However, this teacher said, "That's a good question. What do you think?" After the girl replied, "I think so," the teacher said, "That's a great guess. Now where do you think they would be?" She paused, scrunched her face in thought, and said, "I don't know, maybe by the markers?" To which the teacher said, "That's another great guess. Where are the markers?" The girl then turned and pointed toward a box of markers across the room which, coincidentally, was right beside a carton of pencils. It's in those seemingly insignificant moments when educators and parents can unleash creative thinking.

Invention and discovery emanate from being able to try seemingly wild possibilities and work in the unknown; to be comfortable being wrong before being right; to live in the world as a keen observer, with an openness to experiences and ideas; to play with ideas without censoring oneself or others; to persist through dark valleys with a growth mind-set; to improvise ideas in collaboration and conversation with others; and, to have a willingness to be misunderstood, sometimes for long periods of time, despite conventional wisdom.

Frank Gehry was trained in traditional architecture techniques and designed conventional buildings, such as tract homes and shopping malls, for much of his career. Inspired by how artists worked with materials, Gehry performed a series of experiments on his own house in Santa Monica, California, in the late 1970s. He was fifty years old. The money was good in conventional architecture, yet Gehry decided to close down his firm and start anew, using his own style and voice. The most important step was for Gehry to start making little bets.

As the noted technologist and inventor Alan Kay once said, "The best way to predict the future is to invent it." After all, life is a creative process.

It all begins with one little bet. What will yours be?

Further Readings
and Resources

Trade Books

Coyle, Daniel. *The Talent Code*. New York: Bantam, 2009. After months of wrestling with questions about the role of deliberate practice, including reviewing a broad swath of research and literature supporting the now-popularized "10,000-hour" rules, I found Daniel Coyle's book to be surprisingly good. I ultimately decided not to include an additional chapter on the role of deliberate practice, especially given the strength of Carol Dweck's research on mind-sets. Yet Coyle's book is extremely well researched and written, and draws extensively upon neuroscience research about the role of *myelin*, the neural connections that one can develop and strengthen to develop their talents and capacities (like muscles in the brain) for anything from athletics to creative endeavors. One of Coyle's core findings, like Dweck's, was that one must be willing to make lots of mistakes in order to develop talents, that is, myelin neural connections.

Dweck, Carol. *Mindset: The New Psychology of Success*. New York: Random House, 2006. Numerous authors and academics now hail Dweck's research, but her trade book is a gem itself. She draws upon her own research as well as a plethora of other psychology research, and writes in a very accessible manner. This book is a superb introduction to her research as well as an aid to help change one's own mind-set.

Kahney, Leander. *Inside Steve's Brain*. New York: Portfolio, 2009. Kahney, a contributing editor at *Wired* magazine, has done the best job I've seen of writing about Steve Jobs and Apple, a company that is notoriously secretive. Kahney's book provides the reader with a fairly detailed feel for how Jobs works and leads, as well as the best description of Apple's design process that I've seen. The book was bolstered by Kahney's ability to interview Apple's chief designer, Jonathan Ive, among other insiders.

Lamott, Anne. *Bird by Bird: Some Instructions on Writing and Life*. Garden City, NY: Anchor, 1995. Anne Lamott is primarily a prominent American novelist, but this is a nonfiction book in which Lamott describes her writing tactics, especially how to overcome the common fears and barriers writers face. Her key insights, applicable to any creative process, include the importance of writing "shitty first drafts" in the interest of getting ideas out first and worrying about perfection later, and writing only as much as she can see in a one inch by one inch picture frame. That is, chunking writing into extremely manageable pieces. Lamott's openness and advice empowered me (and many others) to work through the inevitable blocks that occur throughout a creative process.

Pink, Daniel. *A Whole New Mind: Why Right Brainers Will Rule the Future*. New York: Riverhead, 2006. Dan Pink does a great job of taking an intriguing idea and extending it into a convincing, well-researched argument. In my opinion, this is Pink's best book. It was also the first broad trade book to bring attention to the importance of the field of design by arguing that our educational systems overemphasize left-brain, analytical skills in a fast-changing world at the expense of right-brain, creative-thinking skills like design.

Price, David. *The Pixar Touch: The Making of a Company*. New York: Knopf, 2008. Price's book is not only a fascinating and comprehensive account of Pixar's evolution from a technology-focused hardware company to a digital animation company, it's one of the best business books I've read. Price, a true historian, uncovers an enormous amount of detail about Pixar's history for a fascinating journey.

Suggested Media

The Comedian, directed by Christian Charles. Burbank, CA: Miramax, 2002. This documentary follows two comedians, Jerry Seinfeld and young comedian Orny Adams, as they create a new act from scratch. The film does an amazing job of shining light on the creative process, including the degree of failure involved, even for Seinfeld. Creative processes follow similar patterns whether in stand-up comedy, Pixar, Frank Gehry, entrepreneurship, etc. The first part is extremely challenging and uncertain, hard work and iteration begin to clarify the problems and opportunities, and then it all comes together as the person gains confidence. This documentary illustrates all of these elements beautifully, using a principal who many assume is a creative genius (Seinfeld), but who really has to work his tail off.

TEDTalks: TED talks are presentations from the annual TED Conference, established to share "ideas worth spreading." There are two TED talks about creativity that I would highly recommend. The first is Sir Ken Robinson's 2006 talk, "Ken Robinson Says Schools Kill Creativity." Robinson, a long-time creativity researcher, educator, and author, encapsulates a number of the central insights from his book, *Out of Our Minds: Learning to be Creative* in this twenty-minute talk, which is one of the most viewed TED talks, approaching 100 million views. http://www.ted.com/talks/ken_robinson_says_schools_kill_creativity.html.

The second talk is about nurturing creativity by Elizabeth Gilbert, in which Gilbert, the author of *Eat, Pray, Love*, describes her creative process and the barriers that can block it. http://www.ted.com/talks/elizabeth_gilbert_on_genius.html.

Research-based Books

Chesborough, Henry. *Open Innovation*. Cambridge, MA: Harvard Business Press, 2003. Professor Chesborough of the Haas School of Business at Berkeley combines years of work within industry (disk-drive manufacturing) with rigorous empirical research. In this book, he coined and helped popularize the notion of *open innovation*, a thought movement that has opened research and development beyond corporate walls significantly.

Christensen, Clayton. *The Innovator's Dilemma*. New York: Collins Business, 2003, and *The Innovator's Solution*, with Michael Raynor. Cambridge, MA: Harvard Business Press, 2003. Professor Christensen of Harvard Business School is one of the corporate researchers whom I most respect. Christensen goes to great pains to consider counterarguments and present rigorous findings. His first book, *The Innovator's Dilemma*, describes common problems that established companies face, especially when the status quo bias prevent managers from innovating. His second book, *The Innovator's Solution*, written with Michael Raynor, explores a framework to solve these problems. That book presents compelling research for why growth pressures cause executives to make big bets, and why they're often a mistake.

Collins, Jim. *How the Mighty Fall*. Jim Collins, 2009. In this book, Collins examines patterns companies tend to follow from success to decline and supports that general arc with rich case studies. The patterns Collins highlights closely resemble the patterns from psychology literature, as well as Clayton Christensen's research in *The Innovator's Solution*. Collins's stages of organizational decline and case studies, such as the risk of big bets, are very insightful.

Collins, Jim and Jerry Porras. *Built to Last*. New York: HarperCollins, 1997. Jim Collins, who would later write *Good to Great*, was a professor at Stanford Business School with Professor Jerry Porras when they wrote this book. It is one of my favorite business books, presenting not necessarily new ideas, but keen insights on the types of corporate culture that last over the long term. It's also Amazon founder and CEO Jeff Bezos' favorite business book, as it is for a host of other business leaders, including eBay's CEO John Donahoe.

Drucker, Peter. *Innovation and Entrepreneurship*. New York: Harper-Collins, 1985. It's almost cliché to recommend something by management guru Peter Drucker, but after reading broadly about innovation and entrepreneurship, I found that the insights in this book were some of the best. Drucker structures this book around a number of key principles about the sources of innovation and entrepreneurship, such as: systemic opportunity analysis, starting small, the importance of simplicity, alignment with incentive and rewards systems, and building from one's personal strengths. That this was written near the outset of the fields is a testament to how rigorously and deeply Drucker wrestled with these questions.

Liker, Jeffrey. *The Toyota Way*. New York: McGraw-Hill, 2004. University of Michigan Professor Jeffrey Liker is a long-time student of Toyota's processes and culture. This book provides an excellent overview of the Toyota Production System, otherwise known as *lean production*. Elements include: problem solving and continuous learning (*genchi* and *genbutsu*), respect for people and partners (*kaizen*), flow processes and pull systems to eliminate waste (*kaizen*), and long-term thinking. This book presents interesting case studies, such as the creation of the Prius, to illustrate fourteen Toyota operating principles. (Dr. W. Edwards Deming, the American management thinker, helped Toyota to develop these principles in post–World War II Japan, at a time when resources were sparse in Japan.) Today, Toyota's operating principles strongly influence everyone from Pixar's president Ed Catmull to Amazon's founder and CEO Jeff Bezos to the rapidly growing field of agile software development.

Rogers, Everett. *Diffusion of Innovations*. New York: Free Press, 1995. This is the definitive research book about how ideas spread. Professor Rogers began by looking at how ideas spread in Iowa farming communities in the 1950s and the field shortly exploded. Field research on diffusion, epidemics, and change yielded theories like stages of idea adoption: early, middle, and late adopters. Insights from this book, edited by Rogers, served as cornerstones for books like *The Tipping Point* by Malcolm Gladwell and *Crossing the Chasm* by Geoffrey Moore.

Sawyer, Keith. *Group Genius: The Creative Power of Collaboration*. New York: Basic Books, 2007. Professor Keith Sawyer of Washington University is a psychologist with a scientific bent who combines rigorous and deep creativity research with accessible storytelling in this book. It puzzles me why Sawyer's work isn't better known. He's deeply fluent in the academic research on creativity and produces compelling research around group creativity, improvisation, and creativity in education. This book is his most accessible. His book *Explaining Creativity: The Science of Human Innovation* is a solid overview of creativity research. His blog is also excellent. http://keithsawyer.word press.com/.

Sternberg, Robert J. *Handbook of Creativity*. New York: Cambridge University Press, 1998. Sternberg edited this handbook on creativity research (mostly related to psychology and cognitive science research) years ago and it remains the bible of sorts for the field.

von Hippel, Eric. *The Sources of Innovation*. New York: Oxford University Press, 1994. Professor von Hippel of MIT puts forward compelling research in this book around the role of lead or active users to source innovations across a range of mostly traditional industries. His research has not garnered as much attention as Professor Clayton Christensen's work, but is just as rigorous and has withstood the test of time well and has become increasingly mainstream. Von Hippel's website provides a host of resources related to his research: http://web.mit.edu/evhippel/www/.

Creativity

Bayles, David and Ted Orland. *Art & Fear: Observations on the Perils (and Rewards) of Artmaking*. Eugene, OR: Capra Press, 1993. Artists routinely recommend this book, especially as one that helps them to understand and cope with fear. The primary insights about the creative process include the importance of persistence, support structures, allowing imperfection before perfecting, and not worrying about being judged by the outside world.

Csikzentmihalyi, Mihaly. *Creativity: Flow and the Psychology of Discovery and Invention*. New York: Harper Perennial, 1997. Professor Csikzentmihalyi (pronounced *chick-sent-me-high*) of Claremont College, formerly of the University of Chicago, is a leading researcher and writer in the fields of creativity and "positive" psychology, that is, psychology that builds from intrinsic human interests. His book *Flow: The Psychology of Optimal Experience* (Harper Perennial, 1991) was a landmark description of how people can attain satisfied and creative states of mind, by doing work that interests them that plays to their natural interests and strengths. This book picks up on Csikzentmihalyi's work on flow based on interviews with ninety-one recognized creative people, ranging from jazz musicians to physicists.

de Bono, Edward. *Lateral Thinking: Creativity Step by Step*. New York: Harper & Row, 1970. Edward de Bono probably has done more to raise the profile of creative methods within the corporate world than anyone else over the past thirty years. *Lateral Thinking* is his cornerstone book, covering topics like suspending judgment, design, and visualization techniques. *Lateral thinking*, by definition, is about getting outside what de Bono calls *vertical thinking* or the notion that there is one path to a solution. De Bono helped popularize divergent and convergent thinking, buzzwords in creativity, since lateral thinking by definition suggests that one should generate many possibilities before narrowing in on one path.

Galenson, David. *Old Masters and Young Geniuses*. Princeton, NJ: Princeton University Press, 2005. Galenson, whom I interviewed and whose work I referred to in this book, is a University of Chicago economist who is also an art lover who has done extensive research into how creators work. He examines various stages of creative development around art, poetry, and novel writing, and this book presents his resulting theories. His central argument is that people are either conceptual innovators (like Mozart) or experimental innovators (like Beethoven) and that conceptual innovators tend to do their best work while they are young, whereas experimental innovators tend to do their best work in their later years. Critics have poked holes in Galenson's arguments by finding exceptions to his age rules, but his general distinction is compelling. What's less clear is what the spectrum between conceptual and experimental innovation looks like at the individual level, as well as whether people can move from conceptual to experimental or vice versa. We did a significant amount of investigation into these questions and found evidence that people can move from conceptual to experimental throughout their lives (like Picasso), but not vice versa. Malcolm Gladwell profiled Galenson's work in an October 20, 2008, *New Yorker* article entitled "Late Bloomers." (www.new yorker.com/reporting/2008/10/20/081020fa_fact_gladwell).

Maeda, John. *The Laws of Simplicity*. Cambridge, MA: MIT Press, 2006. Maeda, formerly an associate director of research at the MIT Media Lab and now president of the Rhode Island School of Design, straddles the worlds of technology and art. A humanist, computer scientist, and designer, Maeda is an artist at heart who makes keen observations about people and the world and connections between fields. This book is his latest. As Steve Jobs and Apple show, simplicity is an essential element of design, and Maeda's insights have helped to advance the importance of simplicity in many fields, including management. (Follow Maeda's Twitter feed [@johnmaeda] for tidbits and observations.)

Stokes, Patricia. *Creativity from Constraint*. New York: Springer, 2006. This is about the role of constraints across an array of disciplines, from art to science to writing to architecture to music to fashion. The importance of constraints resonated with everyone I spoke with, from artists to Frank Gehry to entrepreneurs. Working with no constraints, or no parameters, was unanimously seen as extremely difficult, if not impossible. Stokes' book was the best in-depth assessment of constraints that I have found.

Young, James Webb. *A Technique for Producing Ideas.* Lincolnwood, IL: NTC/Contemporary, 1988. In this short book, former advertising executive James Webb Young describes a process for coming up with new ideas that entails two essential parts: doing a very *deep* dive in the area where one wants to come up with an idea, say an advertising slogan about new shoes, while being curious about a *broad* array of topics. Young then advises people to let the ideas and insights simmer in the subconscious mind, perhaps by going for a walk, showering, or even sleeping on it, so that creative ideas can emerge. It's a simple approach, validated by research, and a number of creative practitioners strongly value this book.

Design Thinking

Brown, Tim. *Change by Design: How Design Thinking Transforms Organizations and Inspires Innovation.* New York: Harper Business, 2009. Tim Brown is the CEO of design consultancy IDEO. Brown expands upon his Harvard Business Review article "Design Thinking" in this book, which I often recommend to people who want to understand the current state of design thinking. Brown also wrote an excellent article about design thinking, with Jocelyn Wyatt, for the *Stanford Social Innovation Review*, entitled "Design Thinking for Social Innovation," that can be found at http:www.ssireview.org/articles/entry/design_thinking_for_social_innovation.

Kelley, Tom. *The Art of Innovation.* New York: Crown, 2007, and *The Ten Faces of Innovation.* New York: Crown, 2006. Tom Kelley, brother of David Kelley, cofounder of the design consultancy IDEO and the Stanford Institute of Design, writes well about design-thinking methods. Kelley comes at design from an accessible vantage point (he's a general manager) and I recommend these books to people trying to familiarize themselves with design thinking.

Martin, Roger. *The Design of Business*. Cambridge, MA: Harvard Business School Press, 2009. Roger Martin, a converted academic who is now dean of the Rotman School, was formerly a strategy consultant with Monitor Group. He brings that mindset to this book to persuasively argue for both the strategic importance of design thinking to organizations as well as for business schools. More on Martin can be found at: http://www.rogerlmartin.com.

Moggridge, Bill. *Designing Interactions*. Cambridge, MA: MIT Press, 2007. Bill Moggridge, a cofounder of IDEO, is now head of Cooper-Hewitt National Design Museum in New York. Moggridge is an industrial designer who richly describes the evolution of design thinking and its influences in this book. It's a fascinating history that includes methods pioneered at Xerox's PARC research center and Apple, as well as people who contributed certain influences to design from different disciplines, including psychology and ethnography. Moggridge tells the stories of countless people upon whose shoulders the field now stands.

Richardson, Adam. *Innovation X*. San Francisco: Jossey-Bass, 2010. Richardson, a long-time innovation consultant and a creative director at frog design, inc., writes in a very practical and strategic way. This book is for those looking for design thinking, strategic frameworks, and methods, supported by case-study experiences.

Entrepreneurship

Belsky, Scott. *Making Ideas Happen*. New York: Portfolio, 2010. Scott Belsky is a former Goldman Sachs banker who traded a finance job for starting a creative consulting firm, Behance, and became an author in order to help companies develop their ideas. Belsky's book is well done, a how-to guide for corporate intrapreneurs, managers, and entrepreneurs to frame creative thinking processes and systems.

Fried, Jason, and David Heinemeier Hansson. *Rework*. New York: Crown, 2010. Fried and Hansson, founders of 37Signals, a web software company, play an important role with web businesses these days: They provide common-sense frameworks to build web businesses in an era that rewards little betting. They take principles from agile software development and apply those to any startup.

Gianforte, Greg, and Marcus Gibson. *Bootstrapping Your Business*. Avon, MA: Adams Media, 2005. Professor Saras Sarasvathy pointed me to this book. It provides a host of concrete and specific tactics for entrepreneurs who want to start businesses completely from scratch, with their own resources, including selling, managing cash, inexpensive PR tactics, and customer service. It constantly reminded me of the entrepreneurs whom we worked with at Summit Partners, which is not entirely surprising, since Greg Gianforte is the founder and CEO of RightNow Technologies, a customer relationship management software company that Summit backed. The book is very insightful for anyone who wants to bootstrap a business.

Yunas, Muhammad, and Alan Jolis. *Banker to the Poor: Micro-Lending and the Battle Against World Poverty*. New York: Public Affairs, 1999. This is an extremely good book for people interested in social entrepreneurship. It illustrates just how much Yunas relied on little bets to identify and solve the problems he did. It's an interesting story, as Yunas moved from economist to entrepreneur.

Strategy & Innovation

Johansson, Frans. *The Medici Effect: Breakthrough Insights at the Intersection of Ideas, Concepts, and Cultures*. Cambridge, MA: Harvard Business School, 2004. Johansson, an entrepreneur and student of creativity and innovation, writes in an accessible way, blending a diverse array of stories together with key insights from creativity psychology research. Johansson brings to life research from Amy Edmondson and Teresa Amabile, among others.

Lafley, A. G., and Ram Charam. *The Game-Changer: How You Can Drive Revenue and Profit Growth with Innovation*. New York: Crown, 1988. This book, written by former Procter & Gamble CEO A.G. Lafley, and Ram Charam, a consultant and thought leader, provides a comprehensive overview of Lafley's innovation philosophy and initiatives while CEO of P&G. This book is very useful for managers and executives in terms of the philosophy and set of frameworks it lays out.

McGrath, Rita Gunther, and Ian C. MacMillan. *Discovery-Driven Growth*. Cambridge, MA: Harvard Business School, 2009. Rita McGrath, a Harvard Business School professor, and Ian MacMillan, a professor at the University of Pennsylvania's Wharton School, wrote a solid book, *The Entrepreneurial Mindset* (2000), that served as a basis for this book. McGrath and MacMillan propose thinking differently about traditional management decision-making models by building income statements up, by determining what revenues need to be achieved to support costs. Their method is similar to what Professor Saras Sarasvathy calls the principle of *affordable loss*. By reframing analyses from what one expects to gain (traditional expected value calculations) to what one can afford to lose, decision making more closely resembles that of expert entrepreneurs.

Ramo, Joshua Cooper. *The Age of the Unthinkable*. New York: Little, Brown, 2009. Ramo, a former foreign editor for *Time*, builds the core argument of his book around complex adaptive systems logic using an array of examples, from Hamas to Google. The ideas about navigating uncertainty are interesting and timely, but Ramo's argument doesn't hang together as well as it could. That said, a number of investors really like this book, particularly those with a macroeconomic or foreign policy bent.

Senge, Peter. *The Fifth Discipline*. New York: Doubleday, 1990. MIT's Peter Senge has been a primary contributor to the thinking behind what it takes to build sustainable and learning organizational cultures. This is Senge's cornerstone book.

Taleb, Nassim Nicholas. *The Black Swan*. New York: Random House, 2007. Academic, researcher, and investor Nassim Taleb's book is an important reminder of the impact of unlikely events. It's a thought-provoking intellectual adventure. One of the points that Taleb highlights is that, when operating within a high degree of uncertainty, one should experiment including to find what Taleb calls *inadvertent discoveries*. Countless innovations have happened this way, including Alexander Fleming's discovery of penicillin, which he found in a mold that had contaminated another experiment.

Thomke, Stefan. *Experimentation Matters*. Cambridge, MA: Harvard Business School, 2003. Thomke had done valuable work on business experiments, especially within technology. He focuses on industries like integrated circuits, and presents impressive research about approaches to developing ideas that are experimental in their nature, including the role of modeling and simulation technologies like CAD to aid in that process. Thomke's suggested processes, in fact, share a great deal in common with the ones described in this book or from the military OODA models: design, build, run, analyze, that is, learn by experimenting. He shines light on new venture costs, time, fidelity of experiments, capacities, and so on with specific examples from BMW, Eli Lilly, and others.

Tushman, Michael L., and Charles O'Reilly. *Winning Through Innovation*. Tushman, a professor at Harvard Business School and O'Reilly, a professor at Stanford Business School, argue that organizations must be able to both create operational efficiencies as well as explore new areas. Doing both effectively at the same time poses one of the most significant challenges and problems throughout the organizational behavior research. The authors, therefore, propose that organizations should aim to be ambidextrous, capable of doing both by having in essence two distinct cultures. IBM is a central example and the approach has a number of adherents.

von Clausewitz, Carl. *On War.* Researching the military and the various internal debates around conventional versus creative thinking, *On War* (1832) is consistently referenced by counterinsurgency strategies. Written by Prussian militarist Carl von Clausewitz in response to Napoleon's rise, it chronicles the factors that can impact the outcome of war. One of the main reasons for this is that the book describes the complexities of warfare, particularly for its many and unpredictable human elements, in a way that has compelled military leaders for centuries. The *fog of war* appears throughout these references and von Clausewitz appears to be an extremely compelling reference throughout the ranks.

Suggested Twitter Feeds

@brainpicker Feed of Maria Popova, a writer for *Wired* and *Good Magazine* and keen observer of culture, innovation, and creative trends.

@ConanOBrien Comedians have taken to Twitter strongly as a way of developing a direct connection to their audience as the media world disintermediates (in this way, comedy leads other people and industries). O'Brien's feed is my favorite, although there are many others to watch experiment, including CBS's Craig Ferguson (@CraigyFerg) and Tina Fey (@TinaFey123) of *Saturday Night Live* and *30 Rock* fame.

@frogdesign Frog design is a leading design consultancy and their Twitter feed is often very good, packed with content on design and innovation that its staff finds useful.

@gruber   John Gruber has a great eye for insightful stories across creativity, design, technology, and business. He also maintains the blog for Parsons The New School for Design called Daring Fireball: http://daringfireball.net/, with stories updated regularly.

@harvardbiz   Ideas from business world, including entrepreneurship, innovation, design, and creativity.

@ideo   Information and ideas from IDEO, a leading design consultancy, including an aggregation of insights from individual Twitter accounts of IDEO staff, including the company's CEO, Tim Brown. (See also Core77, a design magazine)

@nntaleb   Nassim Taleb, author of *The Black Swan* and hedge fund investor, shares his thoughts about decision making amid uncertainty.

@orenjacob   If you're curious about Pixar, Oren Jacob is the company's chief technology officer and a frequent tweeter. You can also follow Ed Catmull (@edcatmull), even though he's a less frequent tweeter. Or, there's *Toy Story 3* director Lee Unkrich (@leeunkrich) or long-time Pixar storyboard artist Jeff Pidgeon (@jpidgeon).

@techcrunch   TechCrunch (www.techcrunch.com) is a top technology blog. With millions of RSS subscribers and fast-moving editors (@arrington and @erick schonfeld), it has often struck me how TechCrunch leads other information providers on trends and ideas, especially around entrepreneurship and innovation.

@sirkenrobinson   Sir Ken Robinson is one of the leading voices about creativity in education. If you like his TED talk, you'll enjoy following him on Twitter.

@stanforddschool   The Stanford d.school feed. See also: www.dschool.stanford.edu.

@the99percent Consistently relevant and practical insights from Behance, the innovation and creative consultancy founded by Scott Belsky, who is also author of *Making Ideas Happen*.

@ycombinator Y Combinator is an innovative group that has significantly influenced the Silicon Valley venture capital and entrepreneurship community. It gives talented young people, typically twenty-somethings, about $25,000 in exchange for small equity ownership positions, then facilitates regular seminars for those people with insightful people, such as execs at Google or thought leaders. Y Combinator, therefore, makes little bets and has received investments from traditional VCs, such as Sequoia, who hope to access its entrepreneurs and thinking. This feed contains lots of insights.

Notes

Introduction

Stand-up comedy: Discussions with stand-up comedians, including two interviews with Matt Ruby about Chris Rock's approach to small club performances. Rock's quote about "training camp" and Stress Factory reference taken from: "Chris Rock on Obama's Win: It's Good for White Kids, too," by Barry Koltnow, *Orange County Register*, November 5, 2008. Other sources: "Hard at Work on New Year's Eve," by David Carr, *New York Times*, December 28, 2007; Chris Rock appearance on *Tavis Smiley*, PBS, April 2010. Insights about Jerry Seinfeld taken from *The Comedian*, a documentary directed by Christian Charles, with Jerry Seinfeld, 2002. *The Onion* headlines creative process: special thanks to Stanford Professor Robert Sutton's blog *Work Matters:* "Generating 600 Ideas to Get 18: Failing Forward at The Onion." Sutton's source: an episode of *This American Life* called "Tough Room," notably "Act One: Make 'em Laff," originally aired February 2008.

Google's early history: Further information about Google's emergence from a Stanford Integrated Digital Library Project funded by the National Science Foundation (NSF) can be found in an August 17, 2004 NSF article entitled, "On the Origins of Google," which can be found at: http://www.nsf.gov/discoveries/disc_summ.jsp?cntn_

id=100660. Stanford University President and Google Director John Hennessy relates the connection between the Digital Library Project algorithm and Google's core algorithm in a February 19, 2009 lecture entitled, "Innovation as the Crux of Entrepreneurship," as part of the Entrepreneurial Thought Leader Series, which can be found at: http://ecorner.stanford.edu/authorMaterialInfo.html?mid=2111. Google AdWords business model evolution derived from *Inside Larry and Sergey's Brain* by Richard L. Brandt, Portfolio (2009), 96–100.

Amazon: Fifteen discussions with current or former Amazon employees and industry analysts. Secondary sources included: "Institutional Yes: The HBR Interview with Jeff Bezos," by Julia Kirby and Thomas Stewart, *Harvard Business Review*, October 2007; "Jeff Bezos: 'Blind-Alley' Explorer," by Robert Hof, *BusinessWeek*, August 19, 2004; "What's Dangerous Is Not to Evolve," by Michael Schick, *Fast Company*, February 17, 2009; "The Customer Is Always Right: Jeff Bezos," by Daniel Lyons, *Newsweek*, December 21, 2009; "Amid the Gloom, an E-Commerce War," by Brad Stone, *New York Times,* October 11, 2008; "Amazon Auctions Losing Momentum to eBay," by Troy Wolverton, *ZD Net News*, August 2001; "Amazon, Sotheby's Closing Jointly Operated Auction Site," by Troy Wolverton, *CNET News*, October 10, 2000; "Amazon.com Whiz Jeff Bezos Keeps Kindling Hot Concepts," by Patrick Seitz, *BusinessWeek*, December 31, 2009; and Amazon.com, Inc. Earnings Call Transcripts.

Conceptual versus experimental innovators: University of Chicago Professor David Galenson, an economist with a passion for art history, has spent years chronicling the creative processes and methods prominent creators use. Galenson puts creators into two distinct categories: conceptual and experimental, which he describes in his book *Old Masters & Young Geniuses*, Princeton (2005). Conceptual innovators, like Pablo Picasso or Mozart, work with certitude and boldness about their ideas, rather than relying upon trial and error as experimental innovators do. As Picasso said in 1923: "I have never made trials or experiments. Whenever I had something to say, I have said it in the manner in which it needed to be said . . . I can hardly understand the importance given to the word research in connection with modern painting. In my opinion to search means nothing in painting. To find is the thing." Conceptual innovators tended to be what we think of as prodigies. Experimental innovators, in Galenson's terminology, like Mark Twain or Cézanne, meanwhile work as if they are constantly searching. "Their goals are imprecise, so their procedure is tentative and incremental," Galenson writes. As Cézanne said: "I seek in painting."

My research team and I examined Galenson's conceptual/experimental distinction by speaking with Galenson and other creativity experts, as well as by doing significant secondary research. We found the distinctions to be insightful, although we found too many exceptions to the rules to suggest that people are either conceptual or experimental. It's a spectrum. Picasso, for example, acted conceptually when he was young, yet was more experimental later in life. Critics poke holes in the binary model: that people are either conceptual or experimental, or that age is the dependent variable. That said, Galenson's depth of research is rightfully respected and his distinctions map closely to the distinctions between problem solving and problem finding, an established pillar of creativity research (see *Handbook of Creativity* by Robert J. Sternberg, Cambridge University Press [1998]). Our conclusion was that certain types of people are more likely to have an experimental mind-set than others, but that experimental capabilities are both achievable and additive for anyone, especially since they can be delineated.

Thomas Edison: A number of books chronicle Thomas Edison's work processes. The popular quote about ten thousand failures is from *Encyclopedia Britannica*. The reference to the number of failures required to create the light bulb comes from Laurie Carlson's book *Thomas Edison for Kids: His Life and Ideas*, Chicago Review Press (2006), 116. It should be noted that numerous collaborators supported Edison.

Beethoven and Mozart creative processes: References draw upon general research about Beethoven and Mozart, such as the *Encyclopedia of the Romantic Era, 1760–1850*, vol. 1, by Christopher John Murray,

Notes

Fitzroy Dearborn (2004), as well as discussions with David Galenson, a story in the *International Herald Tribune*, "Beethoven Manuscript, Lost 115 years, Is Found." Those who have studied the manuscripts of both Mozart and Beethoven observe interesting differences between the two. Here's one example, from Yale University Professor Craig Wright, a music historian, comparing the two in a lecture for his Listening to Music course:

> Inexhaustible melodic supply, fecundity of imagination when it comes to melody. This is an interesting thing. It's something I'm studying in my own work at the moment, looking at a lot of Mozart's sketches. And Mozart sometimes would have to sketch something. He'd sometimes get in a little bit of trouble and have to write something. For the most part, he had it all in his head—he was just writing it down—but sometimes he did have to sketch things. When he gets in trouble and has to sketch it's contrapuntal issues, never melody.
>
> Now you look at Beethoven's sketches in the Beethoven sketch books and Beethoven will wrestle with trying to craft or get this melody exactly the way he wants it over and over again, erasure after erasure. When you look at the Beethoven section of the textbook there, there's a facsimile of—out of the second movement of the Beethoven Fifth Symphony. Notice all the erasures there and the constant corrections. It took him about twenty years before he was happy with [plays piano, "Ode to Joy"]. He worked on that thing for a long, long time before he got it exact. That would never happen with Mozart. This just flowed perfectly.

Bill Gates and bednets: Interview with David Galenson and "Colin Powell and Bill Gates Join Malaria Campaign," by Alex Dobuzinskis, *Reuters*, April 21, 2010.

Hewlett and Packard: *The HP Way: How Bill Hewlett and I Built Our Company*, by David Packard (Collins), 1996, 39.

Notes

Dr. Saras Sarasvathy: Drawn from discussion with Professor Sarasvathy, as well as from the following secondary sources: "What Makes Entrepreneurs Entrepreneurial?" by Saras Sarasvathy, University of Washington (2001), as referenced by Khosla Partners: http://www .khoslaventures.com/khosla/entrepreneurial.html. "The Entrepreneurial Method: How Expert Entrepreneurs Create New Markets," by Saras D. Sarasvathy, associate professor of business administration, Darden School of Business, University of Darden School Foundation, 2006. "New Venture Performance," by Saras D. Sarasvathy, University of Darden School Foundation, 2006. *Effectuation: Elements of Entrepreneurial Expertise* by Saras Sarasvathy (Edward Elgar Publishing), 2008.

Howard Schultz and Starbucks: Derived from *Pour Your Heart Into It: How Starbucks Built a Company One Cup at a Time* by Howard Schultz and Dori Jones Yang (Hyperion), 1999, and "The Entrepreneurial Method: How Expert Entrepreneurs Create New Markets," by Saras D. Sarasvathy, Associate Professor of Business Administration, Darden School of Business; University of Darden School Foundation, 2006. Sarasvathy uses the Starbucks case as an example of how it's often impossible to predict the future based on current or past information, in Starbucks' case, the growth of the U.S. coffee market.

Abductive and deductive thinking: American philosopher Charles Sanders Peirce, a logic theorist, originally developed the distinctions between deduction, abduction, and induction. Roger Martin, Dean of the Rotman School of Business, and a design thinking and business thought leader, does a very good job of explaining the differences between these modes of thought in *The Design of Business: Why Design Thinking is the Next Competitive Advantage*, Harvard Business School Press, 2009. See Introduction and chapter 1.

Right brain, left brain analogies: Although these analogies have become a popular way to delineate different types of thinking, neuroscientists and brain science practitioners are quick to point out that the creative functions of the brain occur throughout the brain, particularly in the frontal lobes. For a practical overview of neuroscience research and related applications, see *The Sharp Brains Guide to Brain Fitness: 18 Interviews with Scientists, Practical Advice, and Product Reviews, to Keep Your Brain Sharp* by Alvaro Fernandez and Elkhonon Goldberg, self-published (2009). It describes what neuroscientists commonly refer to as the *executive functions* of the brain, a broadly accepted framework among neuroscientists compared to what is perceived as the clichéd left-brain, right-brain distinctions. *Charlie Rose: The Brain Series*, a ten-part series on the brain, is also instructive. It can be found at: http://www.charlierose.com/view/collection/10702.

Scientific (or industrial) management: Scientific management originated in the early 1900s, exemplified by *The Principles of Scientific Management*, by Frederick Taylor, Harper & Brothers (1911), a seminal book. Henry Ford's brand of industrial management (Fordism) drew upon similar methods and techniques: *The Legend of Henry Ford* by Keith Sward, Rinehart & Company (1948).

General Motors: Interview with Chet Huber. See also *My Years with General Motors*, reprinted by Alfred Sloan, Crown Business (1990). Stanford Professor Robert Sutton, an organizational behavior specialist, has studied and interacted with GM for years and shares key insights in the blog post: "The Auto Industry Bailout: Thoughts About Why GM Executives Are Clueless And Their Destructive 'No We Can't' Mindset," which can be found at: http://bobsutton.typepad.com/my_weblog/2008/11/the-auto-industry-bailout-thoughts-about-why-gm-executives-are-clueless-and-their-no-we-cant-mindset.html, as well as: "Is GM's Culture Really Changing, Or Is It Just More Hot Air?" which can be found at http://bobsutton.typepad.com/my_weblog/2008/11/the-auto-industry-bailout-thoughts-about-why-gm-executives-are-clueless-and-their-no-we-cant-mindset.html. Background on OnStar: "OnStar: Connecting to Customers Through Telematics," *Stanford Business School Case GS-38*, 2004.

Notes

Chapter 1

Ned Barnholt and big bets: Interview with Barnholt. HP sixty year compounded annual growth rate reference from Barnholt discussion as well as from "Garage Gives Birth to Measurement Giant" by John Minck and Barry Manz, *Microwaves & RF,* August 2001. Faced with the need for large chunks of revenue growth, big bets are a mistake that corporate managers repeatedly make, consistent with the empirical findings in *The Innovator's Dilemma* by Clayton Christensen, Collins Business (2003), and *The Innovator's Solution* by Clayton Christensen and Michael Raynor, Harvard Business, 2003. Jim Collins presents similar insights in *How the Mighty Fall,* self-published (2009). "Achieving failures" reference taken from interview with Eric Ries.

West Point education programs and evolution in military thinking and training: Interviews with Colonel Casey Haskins, Major Donald Vandergriff, and Brigadier General H.R. McMaster. Robert McNamara sources: *Fog of War: Eleven Lessons from the Life of Robert S. McNamara,* a documentary by Errol Morris, Sony Pictures Classics (2003). *In Retrospect: The Tragedy and Lessons of Vietnam* by Robert S. McNamara with Brian VanDeMark, First Vintage Books (1995). *On War* by Carl von Clausewitz (1832). Additional resources: *US Army Field Manual (FM) 5-0, The Operations Process,* Headquarters Department of the Army, March 2010. *The U.S. Army/Marine Corps Counterinsurgency Field Manual* by General David Petraeus, et al., University of Chicago Press (2007). "No 'Approved Solutions' in Asymmetric Warfare: Nurturing Adaptive Leaders in an Outcomes-Based Training Environment," by Major Chad Foster, *Assembly,* July–August 2009. *Raising the Bar: Creating and Nurturing Adaptability to Deal with the Changing Face of War* by Donald Vandergriff, Center for Defense Information Press, 2006. "Military Science S330: Teaching through Adaptive Leader Methodology (ALM) and Outcomes Based Training and Education" (course materials) by Major Chad Foster and Major Craig Gibson. "Military Science Instruction at West Point: Using the Adaptive Leader Methodology to Develop Leaders in an OBT&E Environment," by Major Chad Foster, course director

MS300, Department of Military Instruction, United States Military Academy. "Unleashing Design: Planning and the Art of Battle Design," by Brigadier General (P) Edward C. Cardon, U.S. Army, and Lieutenant Colonel Steve Leonard, U.S. Army, *Military Review*, March–April 2010. "The Art of Design: A Design Methodology," by Colonel Stefan J. Banach, U.S. Army, and Alex Ryan, Ph.D., *Military Review*, March–April 2009. "Systematic Operational Design: Learning and Adapting in Complex Missions," by Brigadier General Huba Wass de Czege, U.S. Army, Retired, *Military Review*, January–February 2009. "From Tactical Planning to Operational Design," by Major Ketti Davison, U.S. Army, *Military Review*, September–October 2008.

Saras Sarasvathy: "What Makes Entrepreneurs Entrepreneurial?" by Saras Sarasvathy, University of Washington (2001). "The Entrepreneurial Method: How Expert Entrepreneurs Create New Markets," by Saras D. Sarasvathy, Associate Professor of Business Administration, Darden School of Business, University of Darden School Foundation (2006).

Additional entrepreneurial thinking: "How Entrepreneurs Craft Strategies That Work," by Amar Bhide, *Harvard Business Review*, March–April 1994. "Discovery-Driven Planning," by Rita Gunther McGrath and Ian C. MacMillan, *Harvard Business Review*, July–August 1995.

Pixar: Historical references drawn from *The Pixar Touch* by David Price, Knopf (2008). Steve Jobs invested $10 million total to buy Pixar, $5 million went to George Lucas and $5 million in growth capital for the company. "Pixar Can't seem to Animate Itself," *San Francisco Chronicle*, March 29, 1991. *The Second Coming of Steve Jobs*, Alan Deutschman, Broadway Books (2000), 118–121.

Interestingly, before Ed Catmull hired him, John Lasseter was actually fired from Disney. As Price chronicles, after Lasseter got his start as an animator at Disney, he became captivated by computer-generated animation when he saw work being done for the movie *Tron*, in 1981. Unlike traditional hand animation, computers allowed animators to work all around objects. It was three-dimensional. "I couldn't believe what I was seeing," he would later say. "Walt Disney all his career, all his life, was striving to get more dimension in his animation . . . I was standing there, looking at it, going, 'This is what Walt was waiting for.' " Lasseter's subsequent efforts to develop computer animation projects went virtually nowhere within Disney's then risk-averse and rigid culture. "It fell on deaf ears," he said in a speech. "I was told [Disney executives] were only interested in computer animation if it could make [traditional animation] better and cheaper." Lasseter felt stymied. "It was like my heart was ripped out," he recalled. "This was not what I always dreamed Disney was."

However, one Disney executive, Tom Wilhite, the head of live-animated production (and a rare risk taker) agreed to give Lasseter $60,000 to direct a thirty-second computer animated test film based on Maurice Sendak's book *Where the Wild Things Are*. Once completed, the ambitious Lasseter then tried to take a further step to develop an idea to combine hand animated characters with some computer-animated sets for a story called *The Brave Little Toaster*. While he secured Wilhite's support again, Lasseter's superiors quickly rejected the idea. Minutes later, Lasseter got a call from a manager saying: "Since it's not going to be made, your project at Disney is now complete. Your position is terminated, and your employment with Disney is now ended." Ironically, Disney executives would soon spend years trying to recruit Lasseter back, but he would become Disney's chief creative officer only after the company bought Pixar for $7.4 billion in 2006.

Hewlett-Packard calculators: Interview with Chuck House, a longtime HP veteran and HP historian, the coauthor with Raymond Price of *The HP Phenomenon*, Stanford Business Books (2009).

Chapter 2

Vinod Khosla "fail in every possible way": Quote from "How to Succeed In Silicon Valley by Bumbling and Failing . . ." by Tom Foreminski, *Silicon Valley Watcher*, June 28, 2009.

Research on mind-sets: Interview discussions with Dr. Carol Dweck and the following secondary sources: *Mindset: The New Psychology of Success* by Carol Dweck, Random House (2006). "Implicit Theories of Intelligence Predict Achievement Across an Adolescent Transition: A Longitudinal Study and an Intervention," by Lisa S. Blackwell, Kali H. Trzesniewski, and Carol Dweck, *Child Development*, 78, 246–263. "Caution: Praise Can Be Dangerous," *American Educator*, Spring 1999. "Children's Implicit Personality Theories as Predictors of Their Social Judgments," by Cynthia A. Erdley and Carol Dweck, *Child Development*, 1993, 64, 863–878. "The Effects of Praise on Children's Intrinsic Motivation: A Review and Synthesis," (a meta-analysis) by Jennifer Henderlong and Mark R. Lepper, *Psychological Bulletin*, 2002, vol. 128, 5, 774–795. "The Perils and Promises of Praise," by Carol Dweck, *Early Intervention at Every Age*, vol. 65, 2, 34–39. For a good general overview of Dweck's research and related reactions: "How Not to Talk to Your Kids," by Po Bronson, *New York Magazine*, February 11, 2007, which can be found at: http://nymag .com/news/features/27840/.

Michael Jordan: "Jordan's interview with John Thompson," *Sports Illustrated*, February 4, 2003.

Pixar: Ed Catmull comments about disagreeing with him when he's wrong, validated by discussions with Pixar employees on background, taken from a *Harvard Business Review* podcast interview, "Pixar's Collective Genius," August 2008, which can be found at: http:// blogs.hbr.org/hbr/hbreditors/2008/08/how_pixars_ed_catmull_em powers.html. Brad Bird references drawn from *McKinsey Quarterly* interview: "Innovation lessons from Pixar: An interview with Oscar-winning director Brad Bird" by Stanford Professors Robert I. Sutton and Huggy Rao, along with Allen Webb, April 2008, which can be found at: http://www.mckinseyquarterly.com/innovation_les sons_from_Pixar_An_interview_with_oscar_winning_director_Brad_ Bird_2127. Historical references, including *Toy Story 2* crisis, drawn from *The Pixar Touch* by David Price, Knopf (2008). Other references including "Going from Suck to Non-Suck," "success hides problems," and historical references taken from Ed Catmull lecture at Stanford's Computer Science School, April 2010. Other references drawn from: "Curious at Amazon, but Not Idle" by Saul Hansell, *New York Times Bits*, March 27, 2009; "Drawn Together at Pixar," by David Cohen, *Variety*, September 2008; "How Pixar Fosters Collective Creativity," by Ed Catmull, *Harvard Business Review*, September 2008; and, interview with Pete Docter and visits to Pixar Headquarters in Emeryville, California.

Frank Gehry: Interview with Gehry. *Sketches of Frank Gehry*, a documentary film by Sidney Pollack, Sony Pictures (2006).

Chapter 3

Forms of Perfectionism: "Positive conceptions of perfectionism: Approaches, Evidence, Challenges," by Joachim Stoeber and Kathleen Otto, *Personality and Social Psychology Review* 10, 295–319. "Perfectionistic concerns suppress associations between perfectionistic strivings and positive life outcomes," by Robert Hill, Timothy J. Huelsmana and Gustavo Araujoa, *Personality and Individual Differences*, vol. 48, 5, April 2010, 584–589. "The Two Faces of Perfectionism," by Tom Jacobs, *Miller-McCune*, January 28, 2010.

Andrew Stanton reference: Stanton, Pixar Director of *Finding Nemo* and *WALL-E*, is well-known around Pixar for talking about the importance of "failing quickly to learn fast." Other directors there, like Pete Docter, quote him. Quote taken from an interview Stanton did with Slashfilm, about nine minutes into the discussion, which can be found at: http://www.slashfilm.com/37-minute-interview-with-andrew -stanton/. Stanton also spoke about the topic during an extended, oral history discussion of Pixar at the Computer History Museum in San Jose in March 2005. Others on the panel included Pixar founder and president, Ed Catmull, cofounder Alvy Ray Smith, and director Brad Bird.

Anne Lamott: Novelist Anne Lamott details her creative process in her book *Bird by Bird: Some Instructions on Writing and Life*, Anchor, 1995. Lamott says that she only knows of one novelist who acknowledges working this way: English novelist Muriel Spark. "She felt so plugged into God and into 'the plan' that she felt like she had Dictaphones on," Lamott related. Lamott's own experiences and observations of the work process of other novelists differ. "I would almost guarantee that every writer you love and every work that writer you love began as a really shitty first draft and the person was just tortured and degraded by the experience of bringing the book home," Lamott said at an appearance at City Arts & Lectures on April 19, 2010, San Francisco, California.

Frank Gehry: Interview with Gehry. *Sketches of Frank Gehry*, a documentary film by Sidney Pollack, Sony Pictures (2006).

Obama new media team: Visit to campaign headquarters and follow-up interview with Joe Rospars.

Pixar storyboarding: Drawn from visits to Pixar Corporate Headquarters in Emeryville, California, where figures about the number of storyboards used per film are listed, an interview with Director Pete Docter, as well as Joe Ranff quote from Pixar's website, which features a section called "How We Do It," which can be found at: www.pixar.com/howwedoit). Ed Catmull quote taken from lecture at Stanford's Computer Science School, April 2010.

***Finding Nemo* crisis:** Detail on *Finding Nemo* crisis on DVD, director's commentary from Andrew Stanton. Michael Eisner's assessment from *The Pixar Touch* by David Price, Knopf (2008), p. 23. Great assessment on crisis from Jim Hill's blog *Jim Hill Media*, "How Pixar fixed *Finding Nemo*," which can be found at: http://jimhillmedia.com/editor_in_chief1/b/jim_hill/archive/2008/01/29/toon-tuesday-how-pixar-fixed-finding-nemo.aspx?PageIndex=2. Ed Catmull sentiment taken from aforementioned *Harvard Business Review* podcast interview, "Pixar's Collective Genius," August 2008.

Notes

Procter & Gamble: Interviews with P&G executives Chris Thoen and Karl Ronn, as well as discussions with Stanford d.school P&G collaborators. Results drawn from *The Game-Changer* by A.G. Lafley and Ram Charan, Crown Business (2008).

Chapter 4

Frank Gehry: *Sketches of Frank Gehry*, a documentary film by Sidney Pollack, Sony Pictures (2006).

Charles Limb's fMRI study and related research and reactions: "Neural Substrates of Spontaneous Musical Performance: An fMRI Study of Jazz Improvisation," by Charles Limb and Allen R. Braun, *PLoS ONE*, 3 (2), February 2008. Experiences that spark creativity: "Aha! Insight Experience Correlates with Solution Activation in the Right Hemisphere," by Edward Bowden and Mark Jung-Beeman, *Psychonomic Bulletin & Review*, 2003, 10 (3), 730–737. "Smart Babies," by Jonah Lehrer, on Lehrer's blog *The Prefrontal Cortex*, which can be found at: http://scienceblogs.com/cortex/2010/07/smart_babies.php. Brain during REM cycles: "Regional Cerebral Blood Flow throughout the Sleep-Wake Cycle," by A. R. Braun, T. J. Balkin, N. J. Wesenten, R. E. Carson, M. Varga, P. Baldwin, S. Selbie, G. Belenky, and P. Herscovitch, *Brain*, vol. 120, 7, 1173–1197. "Creation on Command," by Jonah Lehrer, *SEED Magazine*, May 6, 2009.

The improvising brain: "The Improvising Brain: Getting to the Neural Roots of the Musical Riff," by Lesley Bannatyne, *Harvard Science*, February 2009. "Generation of Novel Motor Sequences: The Neural Correlates of Musical Improvisation," by Aaron Berkowitz, a Harvard graduate student in ethnomusicology, and Dr. Daniel Ansari, a psychology professor at the University of Western Ontario, published in *NeuroImage*, 41, 2008, 535–543; it received the journal's 2008 Editor's Choice Award in Systems Neuroscience. Attribution to Berkowitz about creative muscle: taken from appearance on the television program *Charlie Rose* on July 15, 2010, which can be found at: www.charlierose.com/guest/view/6944. Other reference: "People Thinking about Thinking People: The Role of the Temporo-Parietal Junction in "Theory of Mind," by R. Saxe and N. Kanwisher, *NeuroImage*, vol. 19, 2003, 1835–1842.

Flow and Mihaly Csikszentmihalyi research. Interview with Csikszentmihalyi. "Go with the Flow," by John Geirland, *Wired*, September 1996. *Flow: The Psychology of Optimal Experience* by Mihaly Csikszentmihalyi, Harper Perennial (1991). *Creativity: Flow and the Psychology of Discovery and Invention* by Mihaly Csikszentmihalyi, Harper Perennial (1997).

Improvisation illustrations: Drawn from personal experiences taking an improvisation class.

Plussing at Pixar: How Pixar teaches plussing using techniques from improvisation: Randy Nelson, former dean of Pixar University, the company's in-house learning unit, "Learning and Working in the Collaborative Age," talk at Edutopia, September 2010. Victor Navone quotes drawn from "Inside Dailies at Pixar: Expressing Your Opinion About Changes in Animation" by Victor Navone, *Animation Mentor Newsletter*, September 2009. Additional detail on Pixar creative process from interviews with Pixar employees, including Pete Docter, director of *Monsters Inc.* and *Up,* including John Lasseter quote about films not ever being finished, just released. Pixar website also has some good additional details at: http://www.pixar.com/artistscorner.

Effects of humor and laughter: Selection of insights taken from meta-analysis of psychology research: "Humor and Group Effectiveness," by Eric Romero and Anthony Pescosolido, *Human Relations,* March 2008, 395–418. *Correlations between humor and trust:* "The Relationship between Humor and Trust," by W. P. Hampes, *Humor,* 1999, 12, 253–9. "Relation between Humor and Empathic Concern," by W. P. Hampes, *Psychological Reports,* 2001, 88, 241–4. "Toward a Sense of Organizational Humor: Implications for Organizational Diagnosis and Change," by W. Kahn, *The Journal of Applied Behavioral Science,* 1989, 25, 45–63. "Cognitive Appraisals and Individual Dif-

ferences in Sense of Humor: Motivational and Affective Implications,"
by N. A. Kupier, S. D. McKenzie, and K. A. Belanger, *Personality and
Individual Differences,* 1995, 19, 359–72. "Humor and Creativity: A
Review of the Empirical Literature," K. O'Quin and P. Derks in, *The
Creativity Research Handbook*, M. A. Runco (ed.), Hampton Press
(1997), 227–56.

HiPPO (Highest Paid Person's Opinion): Discussions with Google
employees as well as comment from Chris Yeh in response to *Harvard Business Review* blog posting: "What Google Could Learn from
Pixar," by Peter Sims, August 6, 2010.

Chapter 5

Frank Gehry: Interview with Gehry. Visits to Disney Hall and Dorothy Chandler Pavilion. "America's Best Leaders: The Man With the
Most Unusual Lines," by Betsy Streisand, *U.S. News and World Report,* October 22, 2006. On feeling lost without constraints: "Interview with Frank Gehry," *Academy of Achievement,* June 3, 1995. On
Disney Hall design and configuration: *Symphony: Frank Gehry's Walt
Disney,* by Frank Gehry, Harry N. Abrams (2003), p 49; "How Frank
Gehry's Design and Lillian Disney's Dream Were Rescued to Create
the Masterful Walt Disney Concert Hall," by James S. Russell, *Architectural Record*, November 2003; Public Broadcasting Services resources: "An Acoustical Tour of Walt Disney Concert Hall," which
can be found at: http://www.pbs.org/wnet/gperf/shows/disneyhall/
disneyhall.htm l.

Marrisa Mayer: "Creativity Loves Constraints," by Marissa Mayer,
Business Week, February 13, 2006.

Constraints: The importance of constraints resonated with nearly
every creative person I spoke with, from artists to Frank Gehry to
entrepreneurs. Constraints are also a core method from the Stanford d.school. Working with no constraints, or no parameters, was
unanimously seen as extremely difficult, if not impossible. Additional

resource: *Creativity from Constraint* by Patricia Stokes, Springer (2006).

Smallifying: Term *smallifying* taken from discussion with Bing Gordon, former chief creative officer of Electronic Arts, now a partner with Kleiner, Perkins, Caulfield & Beyers. Gordon made reference in relation to the software development process and about how developers work better with shorter time frames and smaller teams.

Agile development: A dozen interviews, including with Jeff Sutherland, cofounder of SCRUM Agile methodology, Andre Vanier, as well as visit with Genius.com's agile development teams, as well as other practitioners. Secondary sources: "The Scrum Papers: Nuts, Bolts, and Origins of an Agile Process" by Jeff Sutherland, PhD, and Ken Schwaber (Self-published, 2007). "The New New Product Development Game" by Hirotaka Takeuchi and Ikujiro Nonaka, *Harvard Business Review,* January–February 2006. "Manifesto for Agile Software Development" can be found at: http://agilemanifesto.org/.

Agile methods are not yet mainstream. Companies like Salesforce .com have had successful migrations, while other software companies struggle to implement them. Small teams are critical, as is training and experience with the methods of which there are many variations, including Scrum, Ruby on Rails, Lean Startup, Customer Development Model, and so on. In general, Silicon Valley Internet entrepreneurs use agile methods because they can, and often must given their constraints.

Creativity research on problem finding versus problem solving: Interview with Dr. R. Keith Sawyer, Washington University. *The Creative Vision: A Longitudinal Study of Problem Finding in Art*, by J. W. Getzels and M. Csikszentmihalyi, Wiley (1976). "The Domain of Creativity," by M. Csikszentmihalyi, in *Theories of Creativity*, Mark Runco and Robert S. Albert (eds.), *Sage* (1990), 190–212. Good summary of the Getzels and Csikszentmihalyi research in *Explaining Creativity: The Science of Human Innovation* by R. Keith Sawyer, Oxford University Press (2006). Additional resources: "Problem Finding, problem Solving, and Cognitive Controls: An Empirical Investigation of Critically Acclaimed Productivity," by S. M. Rostan, *Creativity Research Journal*, 1994, vol. 7, 97–110. *Thinking and Learning Skills: Research and Open Questions*, Judith W. Segal, Susan F. Chipman, and Robert Glaser (eds.), Routledge (1985).

Military: Discussions with General H. R. McMaster, as well as other army officials. Secondary sources include: *The U.S. Army/Marine Corps Counterinsurgency Field Manual* by General David Petraeus, et al.; University of Chicago Press (2007). "Letter from Iraq: The Lesson of Tal Afar" by George Packer, *The New Yorker*, April 10, 2006. *Washington Post* reporter Thomas Ricks on raiding: excerpts from NPR interview, January 29, 2007. "The Lessons of Counterinsurgency," by Thomas Ricks, *Washington Post*, February 16, 2006. Statistics from: "Measuring Stability and Security in Iraq," Department of Defense, September 2009.

Chapter 6

Muhammad Yunus and Grameen Bank: Quotations drawn from *Banker to the Poor: Micro-Lending and the Battle Against World Poverty* by Muhammad Yunus and Alan Jolis, PublicAffairs (1999). Special thanks to David Galenson for reference. Quote from Steve Blank taken from Blank's blog, which can be found at http://steveblank .com/2009/09/17/the-path-of-warriors-and-winners/

Military: "Letter from Iraq: The Lesson of Tal Afar" by George Packer, *The New Yorker*, April 10, 2006. "Army Enlists Anthropology in War Zones," by David Rhode, *New York Times*, October 5, 2007. Interview with General McMaster.

Pixar: "Pixar's Bob Peterson: Animator, Screenwriter, Director, Voice Actor, Dog Lover," interview with Glenn Close, *The Huffington Post*, February 14, 2010, which can be found at: http://www.huffington post.com/glenn-close/pixars-bob-peterson-anima_b_460293.html. "How 'Finding Nemo' Works," by Vicki Arkoff, HowStuffWorks, un-

dated, which can be found at: http://entertainment.howstuffworks
.com/how-finding-nemo-works.htm. "Pixar's 'Cars' Got Its Kicks on
Route 66," by Phil Patton, *New York Times*, May 21, 2006.

Dyer and Gregersen research: "The Innovator's DNA," by Jeffrey H.
Dyer, Hal B. Gregersen, and Clayton Christensen, *Harvard Business
Review*, December 2009. "How Do Innovators Think?" by Bronwyn
Fryer, *Harvard Business Review* blog, September 28, 2009, which can
be found at: http://blogs.hbr.org/hbr/hbreditors/2009/09/how_do_in
novators_think.html. Jeff Bezos quote from: "Institutional Yes: The
HBR Interview with Jeff Bezos," by Julia Kirby and Thomas Stewart,
Harvard Business Review, October 2007.

Apple and Steve Jobs: *Inside Steve's Brain*, by Leander Kahney, Portfolio (2008), 190–197. "Steve Jobs: The Next Insanely Great Thing," by
Gary Wolf, *Wired*, March 2002. Steve Jobs calligraphy example taken
from his 2005 Stanford Commencement speech.

James Chanos reference: Interview with Chanos.

Jerry Seinfeld: Drawn from *The Comedian* (DVD), Directed by Christian Charles, with Jerry Seinfeld (2002).

John Legend and Kevin Brereton: Interviews with Legend and
Brereton.

Status quo bias and loss aversion: Origin of status quo bias terminol-
ogy and research: "Status Quo Bias in Decision Making," by William
Samuelson and Richard Zeckhauser, *Journal of Risk and Uncertainty*,
vol. 1, 1988, 7–59. *Addition of loss aversion and endowment effect:*
"The Endowment Effect, Loss Aversion, and Status Quo Bias," by
Daniel Kahneman, Jack L. Knetsch, Richard H. Thaler, *Journal of
Economic Perspectives*, vol. 5, 193–206. "Timid Choices and Bold
Forecasts," by Daniel Kahneman and Dan Lavallo, *Management Sci-
ence*, 39, 17–31.

Notes

Chet Pipkin: Interview with Pipkin.

Procter & Gamble: Interviews with P&G innovation-focused executives Karl Ronn and Chris Thoen. *The Game-Changer: How You Can Drive Revenue and Profit Growth with Innovation* by A.G. Lafley and Ram Charam, Crown Business (1988).

Montessori system: Well-known Montessori graduates drawn from Montessori School websites. Google founders credited their Montessori education as a major factor behind their success in an interview with Barbara Walters, "10 Most Fascinating People of the Year," ABC News, February 2004.

John Lasseter: "Lunch with the FT: John Lasseter," *Financial Times*, January 16, 2009.

Chapter 7

Frank Gehry: Interview with Frank Gehry. *Sketches of Frank Gehry*, a documentary film by Sidney Pollack, Sony Pictures (2006).

Evidence from creativity research about the value of diverse insights: *Individual level:* Openness to experience is one of the foremost characteristics throughout the personality and psychology research on creative people. See *Handbook of Creativity* by Robert J. Sternberg, PhD, Cambridge University Press (1998), 275. *Group level: Group Genius: The Creative Power of Collaboration* by Keith Sawyer, Basic Books (2007), *The Medici Effect: Breakthrough Insights at the Intersection of Ideas, Concepts, and Cultures* by Frans Johansson, Harvard Business School Press (2004). Johansson brings to life research from Amy Edmondson and Teresa Amabile, among others. *Societal level: Regional Advantage: Culture and Competition in Silicon Valley and Route 128*, Harvard University Press (1994) by AnnaLee Saxnian, a University of California, Berkeley professor, describes her fascinating research, which argues that Silicon Valley entrepreneurs are innovative because they interact with more diverse types of people than those working around Boston's Route 128. *The Rise of the Creative Class* by Richard Florida, Basic Books (2002), lays out research and an argument for how diverse cultures are more innovative than homogenous ones. For a good synopsis, see "The Rise of the Creative Class" by Richard Florida, *Washington Monthly,* May 2002, which can be found at: http://www.washingtonmonthly.com/features/2001/0205.florida.html.

Tim Russert secondary sources: "In the Hot Seat: Tim Russert on His Ego, His Bias, His Father Worship and What He Really Thinks about Tax Cuts," by Howard Kurtz, the *Washington Post*, May 23, 2004. "Edwards Admits Sexual Affair; Lied as Presidential Candidate," ABC News, *Nightline*, August 8, 2008. *Meet the Press* transcript, January 22, 2006, NBC News. Senator Barack Obama interview: *Men's Vogue,* September/October 2006.

John Donahoe: Interview with Donahoe.

Management by walking around: Drawn from David Packard's management style at Hewlett Packard, "management by walking around" was popularized by *In Search of Excellence: Lessons from America's Best-Run Companies* by Tom Peters and Bob Waterman, Harper (1982). *Good to Great: Why Some Companies Make the Leap . . . and Others Don't* by Jim Collins, HarperBusiness (2001).

Dr. Richard Wiseman research on luck: *The Luck Factor* by Richard Wiseman, Miramax (2003). Brief summary article: "Be Lucky—It's an Easy Skill to Learn" by Richard Wiseman, *Telegraph*, January 9, 2003, which can be found at: http://www.telegraph.co.uk/technol ogy/3304496/Be-lucky-its-an-easy-skill-to-learn.html

Chapter 8

Diffusion of ideas: *Diffusion of Innovations* by Everett Rogers, Simon & Schuster: Free Press (1995). This is a landmark research book about how ideas spread, edited by Rogers. Professor Rogers began by looking at how ideas spread in Iowa farming communities in the 1950s and the field shortly exploded. Field research on diffusion, epidemics, and change yielded theories like stages of idea adoption: early, middle, and late adopters.

Research from Professor Eric von Hippel: *The Sources of Innovation* by Eric von Hippel, Oxford University Press (1994). Professor von Hippel of MIT puts forward compelling research in this book around the role of lead or active users to source innovations across a range of (mostly) traditional industries. His follow-up book *Democratizing Innovation*, MIT Press (2005), helped form the "open innovation" movement now popular in organizational behavior and innovation research. 3M sources: "Creating Breakthroughs at 3M," by Eric von Hippel, Stefan Thompke, and Mary Sonnack, *Harvard Business Review*, September October 1999. "Breakthroughs to Order at 3M," by Eric von Hippel and Mary Sonnack, MIT-SSM Working Paper, January, 1999. 3M results: "Performance Assessment of the Lead User Generation Process for New Product Development," Lilien, G., Morrison, P.D., Searls, K., Sonnack, M., and Eric von Hippel, *Management Science*, 48 (8), 1042–59. Users, in von Hippel's definition, could be either individuals or organizations. That is, Chris Rock finds active users by picking small comedy clubs dominated by hardcore fans, just as Boeing is a lead user in the aviation industry when it comes to creating new advances in airplanes. Professor von Hippel's website provides a host of resources related to his research: http://web.mit.edu/evhippel/www/

John Legend: Interview with Legend.

Procter & Gamble: Taken from interviews with Chris Thoen, managing director, Global Open Innovation, as well as with George Kembel and colleagues at the Stanford Institute of Design.

SAP reference: Drawn from discussion with Zia Yusef, former executive vice president, Global Ecosystem & Partner Group, SAP. For a good overview article on SAP's ecosystem, see "How SAP Seeds Innovation," by John Hagel and John Seely Brown, *Business Week*, July 23, 2008.

Mountain biking: *Klunkerz: A Film About Mountain Bikes*, Directed by William Savage (2006). Statistics on mountain biking industry from: *We Think: The Power of Mass Creativity* by Charles Ledbetter, Profile (2007).

Chapter 9

Small Wins: "Small Wins: Redefining the Scale of Social Problems," by Karl E. Weick, *American Psychologist*, January 1984, Vol. 39, 1, 40–49. Importantly, Weick credits Tom Peters for providing the original description of "small wins," which Peters wrote about in his 1977 doctoral thesis.

Pixar: Drawn from *The Pixar Touch* by David Price, Knopf (2008).

Howard Schultz and Starbucks: Drawn from *Pour Your Heart Into It: How Starbucks Built a Company One Cup at a Time* by Howard Schultz and Dori Jones Yang.

Agile software: Drawn from previously mentioned agile interviews and see also: "Small Wins: Agile Psychology," by David Churchville, which can be found at: http://www.extremeplanner.com/blog/2007/03/small-wins-agile-psychology.html.

Chapter 10

Alan Greenspan: Quote taken from Congressional testimony from October.

General H. R. McMaster: Drawn from interviews with General McMaster.

Pete Docter: Interview with Docter.

Notes

Richard Tait: Interview with Tait.

Dr. Keith Sawyer: "Educating for Innovation," by R. Keith Sawyer, *Thinking Skills and Creativity*, vol. 1, 41–48.

Classroom: Taken from visit to the Nueva School, I-Lab, an experimental design thinking laboratory for elementary-school students.

Frank Gehry: Interview with Frank Gehry. *Sketches of Frank Gehry*, a documentary film by Sidney Pollack, Sony Pictures (2006).

In Gratitude

Although this book has one author, it stands on the shoulders of countless people whose work, insights, and research inform it. The greatest initial inspiration came from George Kembel, a cofounder and the executive director of the Hasso Plattner Institute of Design at Stanford (the d.school). This book never would have happened without his collaboration and mentoring. The other major source of inspiration came from the hundreds of scrappy entrepreneurs whom I was privileged to observe and work with during my days in venture capital.

The findings featured in this book draw upon the admirable work from an array of scholars and researchers. They include: Robert Burgelman, Clayton Christensen, Carol Dweck, David Kelley, David Galenson, Jeffrey Liker, Everett Rogers, James March, Roger Martin, Keith Sawyer, Robert Sternberg, Robert I. Sutton, Mark A. Runco, and Eric von Hippel. In addition to the interviewees mentioned in the book, the following people volunteered their time and valuable perspectives: Irene Au, Chris Beard, Richard Boly, Thomas Daly, Dawn Danby, Don Frey, Josh Handy, Greg Hawkins, Sam Hinkie, William Huyett, Adam Klein, John Krumboltz, John Lilly, Adam Lowry,

Scott Matthews, Karl Ronn, and Donald Vandergriff. The research began in earnest when a talented group of Stanford students helped turn over a host of initial rocks. They included: Zack Ciesinski, Erik Ehrke, Zinnia Horne, Cyrus Navabi, Matthew Stoltz, Thomas Yeh, and especially Aaron Kofman, Fagan Harris, and Juan Carlos Paredes.

In developing the book, I'm particularly grateful to Christo Sims, Gigi Sims, and John Zapolski for their extensive feedback and insights. Many others provided helpful reactions and advice, including: Ori Brafman, Kheaven Brereton, Alvaro Fernandez, Corey Ford, Elizabeth Gerber, Peter Georgescu, Christopher Gergen, Bing Gordon, Chip Heath, Ryan Jacoby, Kathleen Kelly, Ryan Kiskis, Charles O'Reilly, Lenny Mendonca, Akshata Murty, Leah Rose, Ben Tarbell, and Alan Webber.

As for the rest of the team behind this book, my literary agent, Christy Fletcher of Fletcher & Co., has been a great partner and savvy conspirator, while Don Lamm provided helpful coaching on the proposal and was a reliable sounding board throughout. My editor, Emily Loose, not only got this book and its essential elements from the start, but her patience, perceptive guidance, and stimulating and enjoyable collaboration played a critical role. My enormous thanks also to my Free Press publicist, Christine Donnelly, and to Dominick Anfuso and the entire Free Press team. A final thank you to Mark Fortier for helping to spread the word.

Finally, the best way to predict the future is to invent it, but no one invents a future alone. This book would not have been written without the incredible support (and lots of humor) from my friends and family. I cherish you. Here's to many years of little bets and laughs ahead.

Index

Index

Index

Index

Index

Index

Index

Index

Index

About the Author

Peter Sims is the coauthor with Bill George of the *Wall Street Journal* and *BusinessWeek* bestselling book *True North*. His work has appeared in the *Harvard Business Review*, *Fortune*, and *TechCrunch*, and he is a contributor to the Reuters and Harvard Business Review blogs. He received an MBA from Stanford Business School, where he and several classmates established a popular course on leadership. He has spoken or advised at such organizations as Cisco Systems, Eli Lilly, Current Media, Molson Coors, Qualcomm, and Frost & Sullivan. Previously, Peter worked in venture capital with Summit Partners, a leading investment company, and was part of the team that established the firm's London office.